life as worship

I0807894

Praise for ***Life as Worship***

"John Kitchen has managed to write a powerful, unique and insightful book on worship by exegeting the Psalms of Asaph. Go deeper than a focus on songs and styles and trends, and let this well-written book help you make your life all about worship. You'll be blessed and through you, so will God."

—Dan Adler, Heart of the City Ministries
www.heartofthecity.org

"Here is a book that will go a long way toward solving the real worship war, the war that rages in your own heart. What is worship? *How much* effort should I invest in worship? *When* should I worship? And *what* does real worship look like? Taking his cue from the Psalms, God's own 'order of worship,' John Kitchen confronts us with the reality that *all of life* is worship and can only be properly stewarded with that understanding."

—Tom Elliff
Author of *A Passion for Prayer*

"I read everything that Dr. John Kitchen writes. He is a pastor-scholar who understands the delicate balance between information and transformation. *Life as Worship* continues Kitchen's legacy. After reading this outstanding book, my mind, heart, and feet were motivated to worship the Lord with renewed abandon. Expect to be changed as you read!"

—Keith R. Krell, PhD
Senior Pastor
Fourth Memorial Church, Spokane, WA
Associate Professor, Moody Bible Institute-Spokane

"*Life as Worship* is a refreshing look at how worship is not just something that we do, but it really is our entire life. The book takes the reader on a journey that deepens their understanding of worship and then challenges them to take time to develop a deeper life of worship with practical application. You will not want to just read through it quickly because there is such depth to be explored here!"

—Rev. Derek Mansker
Bethany Alliance Church, Fennimore, WI

"John Kitchen's *Life as Worship* is an outstanding exposition of the Psalms of Asaph. In addition to giving us very able and wise instruction from these biblical songs, Kitchen also writes so excellently, consistently keeping the Scriptural text in our main view. I have been a longtime reader of John Kitchen's writing ministry, including his masterful treatment of Davidic Psalms entitled, *Praying Through*, and now this latest exposition of Asaph's Psalms is surely its worthy companion volume."

—Lance Quinn, Pastor
Grace Advance
Grace Community Church
Sun Valley, CA

life as worship

When Reverence Defines Reality

john kitchen

CLC
PUBLICATIONS
Fort Washington, PA 19034

Life as Worship

Published by CLC Publications

U.S.A.

P.O. Box 1449, Fort Washington, PA 19034

UNITED KINGDOM

CLC International (UK)

51 The Dean, Alresford, Hampshire, SO24 9BJ

© 2015 by John Kitchen

All rights reserved. Published 2015

Printed in the United States of America

ISBN-13 (paperback): 978-1-61958-162-3

ISBN-13 (e-book): 978-1-61958-163-0

Unless otherwise noted, Scripture quotations are from the *Holy Bible, English Standard Version®*, copyright © 2001 by Crossway, a publishing ministry of Good News Publishers. Used by permission. All rights reserved.

Scripture quotations marked KJV are from the Holy Bible, *King James Version,* 1611.

Scripture quotations marked NASB are taken from the *New American Standard Bible®*, © 1960, 1962, 1963, 1968, 1971, 1972, 1973, 1975, 1977, 1995 by The Lockman Foundation. Used by permission.

Scripture quotations marked NIV are from the Holy Bible, *New International Version*, © 1973, 1978, 1984 by International Bible Society. Used by permission of Zondervan Bible Publishers. All rights reserved.

Scripture quotations marked NKJV are from the Holy Bible, *New King James Version*, © 1979, 1980, 1982 by Thomas Nelson, Inc. Used by permission. All rights reserved.

Scripture quotations marked NLT are from the *Holy Bible, New Living Translation*, © 1996. Used by permission of Tyndale House Publishers, Inc., Wheaton, Illinois 60189. All rights reserved.

Scripture quotations marked NRSV are taken from the Holy Bible, *New Revised Standard Version*, © 1989 by the Division of Christian Education of the National Council of Churches of Christ in the U.S.A. All rights reserved.

Italicized words in Scripture quotes are the emphasis of the author.

Dedicated to

Dan Adler

worshiper
leader of worshipers
leader of worship leaders

Table of Contents

Preface

There's a picture in your mind. It's there to greet you as you awaken to the day. It flickers in the nanoseconds between concentrated thoughts as you work. In that nether land between consciousness and sleep, it dances in your subconscious.

That picture determines how you understand and interpret life. It frames your thoughts and seasons your words. It's how you define your interactions and understand your relationships. Like colored lenses, it casts a hue over how you see life and all that fills it.

We live our lives in pictures.

But they are more than mere pictures; they inject meaning into our lives. The pictures are symbols, representing something life-defining and powerful. We pass through each day based on the metaphors in our heads.[1] We each have a primary metaphor through which we interpret life. The metaphor in your head is the standard by which you evaluate your experiences, emote, make choices, choose words, put one foot in front of the other and make it through each day.

How do I know what my metaphor is? It's pretty simple, really. Just finish this sentence: *Life is . . .*

One person might say *life is work.* Another might say *life is leisure.* Someone you know thinks *life is competition.* Yet another believes *life is a party*. Someone else has determined that *life is war.* Their cousin, once removed, believes *life is survival*—just making it through to another day. Someone else demands *life is fulfillment.* Still we could add others, ad infinitum.

Your metaphor reveals itself in every part of your day. Think of your workplace. It isn't difficult to spot the person who pictures life as competition or survival. It shines through their words, their actions and their work ethic. Try being married to a man who concludes *life is leisure* or a woman who lives by the metaphor *life is war!*

There is tremendous, life-defining power in our internal metaphors. Actually, this is by God's intention. God meant us to operate this way. This is why God's Word is filled with word pictures and metaphors to capture our imagination and direct our lives.[2]

That doesn't mean the metaphor in your head was placed there by God. In fact, it may be your metaphor by *default*—based on how your parents raised you. Or it may be yours by *devastation*—how your soul, wounded by some deeply painful experience, has managed to cope with and interpret life. But there is a metaphor that God intends for us to live by. It may not be ours by default or devastation, but was intended to be ours by divine *design* and personal *decision.*

What is this metaphor?

It is simple, but revolutionary; radical because, unlike most of our metaphors, it does not place you at its center. It places God at the heart; of everything.

The most fundamental metaphor for rightly interpreting everything is this: *life is worship*.

How, you may wonder, *do we know this to be our divinely designed metaphor for interpreting, engaging with and living life?*

Two simple facts establish this. First, everything about everything is about the glory of God (see Rom. 11:36). Then also, everything about everything is by the grace of God (see Acts 17:25; 1 Cor. 4:7).[3]

If true (and the Bible tells us they are), these two facts tell us not only something about God, they tell us something about everything else as well. Everything else must conform to the purpose of God's glory. That includes you, me and the choices we make, the thoughts that fill our heads, the words that come from our mouths, the way we do our work, the way we relate to the people in our lives and the leisure we engage in. On the list could go.

If everything about everything is about the glory of God, everything must become an expression of worship. If everything about everything is by the grace of God, then everything is a divine initiative designed to evoke a response of worship.

That is what our lives are called to be: living, unfolding expressions of worship. Not just on Sunday. Not just in the moments we may take each day to read God's Word and pray. Not just in a brief prayer before a meal. Not only when life is going well. Worship is the talking, thinking, driving, working, playing, relaxing. It is the serving, helping, mowing, bathing, buying, selling, eating. *Everything!*

Everything about *everything* must become an expression of worship to God! We are not called merely to weekly worship, periodic worship, rhythmic or seasonal worship. We are called to worship at the speed of *life!*

Sadly, however, many people look at the details and data of life and conclude that such worship simply is impossible. They've chosen to begin with what looks to them like reality and then to determine whether or not God can or should be worshiped. They have chosen to define and limit worship by their experience. If they feel at the moment as if God has blessed them or is doing a commendable job of running the universe, they may be willing to toss some worship His way. If, on the other hand, things aren't turning out to their liking, they withhold said worship.

This is precisely the opposite of life in accord with reality; of life as God intended it. Such people are letting their view of "reality" define their reverence of God. God intends just the reverse—that our reverence define reality. God, rightly worshiped, becomes the lens through which we view all else in life.

God is God, regardless of what may seem to be transpiring around me or within me. I begin with God. I begin with the fact that as Creator and Sovereign over all He has created, He alone possesses the right to be worshiped. I begin with His sovereignty over all things. God is God. Having settled that, I then begin to filter and process the details and data of life through that worldview. The result is that rather than sifting God through my experience and then deciding if I want to worship Him, I give God His rightful place and then measure life by Him. Worship is the only pathway to a sane understanding of life.

This is precisely what the Bible calls for, both early and often. It is the distilled essence of life: "The fear of the LORD is the beginning of knowledge" (Prov. 1:7). Note the order: first, worship ("the fear of the LORD") and only then a right understanding of reality ("the beginning of knowledge"). When it comes to accurately interpreting life, Isaiah was correct, "The fear of the LORD is *the key to this treasure*" (Isa. 33:6, NIV). The "fear of the LORD" is the "first and controlling principle" of life as God intends to deliver it to us.[4]

It is impossible to rightly interpret life unless we begin with *life as worship*. But what would such a life look like? That is the power of metaphor. It engages us by enabling us to see life in a certain way. This book is about how your default, internal, life-defining, mental metaphor can be transformed into the one God intended when He created you. I want to map the way for you to change from *life is* ________ (insert your personal metaphor) to *life is worship*.

Fortunately just such a life is illustrated for us in the Scriptures. And the picture has a face. And the face has a name. That name is Asaph. The profile of his life is depicted for us in the Bible. Asaph's life shows the way. In the chapters that follow, each one taking up one of the psalms that bear Asaph's name, we'll examine the pen strokes that sketch a portrait of *life as worship*.[5] But we're getting ahead of ourselves. Who is this Asaph and why should I care? Why should his life reshape my most basic orientation to life?

Great question! Turn the page, and let's find out.

1

Living a Life of Worship

Life is worship.

Not *should be. Is.*

Humans are worshipers by default. Worship is a reflex. By an inbred necessity of the heart, we adore, sacrifice, praise and give ourselves away in worship. We were created for this.

As A.W. Tozer put it, worship is "the normal employment of moral beings. . . . It is something built into human nature."[1]

The Fall didn't remove the worship impulse; it scrambled it. It didn't obliterate worship; it changed the object of our worship. When Adam and Eve turned from worship of God to devotion to their desires, they cast the mold for all their descendants. John Calvin had it right with regard to the human heart: it is "a perpetual forge of idols."[2] Look around. Look *within*! It's hard to argue with him. Worship is everywhere, idolatrous though much of it is.

Life rightly lived, life fully enjoyed, is lived as an unfolding, moment-by-moment expression of worship *to God.* But what would that *look* like? How am I to *picture* life as worship? The purpose of the pages resting in your hand is to reveal how you can change your internal, default, life-defining, mental metaphor to the one God had in His mind when He created you.

To do that we're going to take up the *discography* of a man named Asaph. That is to say we're going to study the lyrics of a writer of worship songs. We're going to listen in on the prayers of a worshiper of God. So far you know his name. But that's probably about all you know about him. So, before we look at the lyrics, let's examine the lyricist. Before we pray the prayers, let's scrutinize the prayer. Who is this Asaph? Why should I care about him, let alone reshape my most basic orientation to life after the pattern of his own?

Asaph's only credentials—other than the fact that God chose to include him, his story and his prayer-songs in the Bible—is that he lived a life of worship. Life as worship is what we are after, so before we turn to the individual psalms of Asaph, let's study the footprints of one who already walked this road. What do we know about Asaph?

Devoted to Living a Life of Worship

We know from the Bible that *Asaph was a worshiper*. Asaph was devoted to living life as worship. Early on this young man made up his mind concerning what he was created for, what path he would walk and what legacy he would leave.

We first meet Asaph when David was bringing the ark of the covenant from Gibeon to Jerusalem (see 1 Chron. 15). David had prepared a "tent of meeting" in Jerusalem to receive the ark, while leaving the Tabernacle itself in Gibeon.

David previously had attempted to bring the ark up to Jerusalem. Things hadn't gone so well, largely because he'd done so on his own terms rather than treating God as holy—a failure in many ways, but most fundamentally a failure in worship (see 1 Chron. 13). In his first attempt David plopped the ark onto an oxcart, gave the signal and proceeded to roll toward Jerusalem. Along the way one of the oxen staggered. Uzzah reached out a hand to steady the ark.

Bright flash. Fire from heaven. Pile of ash. Smoldering Uzzah.

Not good.

David was angry. Perhaps it was because his self-defined worship was exposed for what it was. In any case he refused to bring the ark into Jerusalem. But the problem was not with his idea of the ark being in Jerusalem. His was a failure in worship. God had previously instructed His people about just *how* the ark was to be handled. David, assuming too much, devised his own means of honoring God rather than allowing God to tell him how He wished to be approached.

Picture, if you will, Asaph as an unnamed extra in the crowd scene. Pause the video and you could imagine him with a clipboard taking notes—*Memo to self: Worship is not a slapdash affair. God must be regarded as holy.*

After three months' time, David's worship reflex couldn't be denied. He determined to try again. This time he followed the instructions in God's Word. Having checked the Scriptures, he'd discovered that the ark must be *carried by* Levites, *not pulled* by oxen.

The Levites received no physical inheritance in the Promised Land. Their inheritance was the privilege of serving the Lord and of helping His people with their expressions of worship. The Levites were in charge of the Tabernacle and later the care of the Temple. Within that tribe, the descendants of Aaron became the priesthood.

Asaph was a Levite (see 1 Chron. 15:17). Asaph was, by virtue of physical descent, a man devoted to living a life of worship.

"Ah," you say, "but worship wasn't his choice! It was the family business! He was born into it."

Precisely! Worship is about lineage and birthright, not primarily about emotion, mood or sentiment.

This side of the cross and resurrection of Jesus, God has made all His children priests! Peter said, "You yourselves like living stones are being built up as a spiritual house, to be a holy priesthood, to offer spiritual sacrifices acceptable to God through Jesus Christ. . . . You are a . . . royal priesthood . . . that you may proclaim the excellencies of him who called you out of darkness into his marvelous light" (1 Pet. 2:5, 9).

No more need of an earthly priest to approach to God! We can all go to God through our High Priest, Jesus Christ! We all serve as priests unto the Lord. If you are a child of God through faith in Christ, you are a priest, not because you *feel* it is true but because you were *reborn* into it. We live lives of worship because it is our birthright as children of God.

Your inheritance is in Christ. "Through him then let us continually offer up a sacrifice of praise to God, that is, the fruit of lips that acknowledge his name" (Heb. 13:15). And, yes, that means you ought to gather with God's people rhythmically, regularly for corporate expressions of that worship: "Not neglecting to meet together, as is the habit of some, but encouraging one another, and all the more as you see the Day drawing near" (10:25).

But it means a good deal more. It means the whole of your life is to be offered up as an expression of worship to God. Not just Sunday morning singing, Bible reading, prayer and offerings. Worship is so much more than church; it is *life*.[3]

Asaph, as a Levite, devoted the whole of his life to making sure God was rightly magnified in himself and in all God's people. Our calling is no less demanding: "And whatever you do, in word or deed, do everything in the name of the Lord Jesus, giving thanks to God the Father through him" (Col. 3:17).

Asaph's name means "gatherer."[4]

What did he gather?

Worshipers!

Asaph's entire orientation to life was to recruit people as worshipers of God. This too is our purpose. A.W. Tozer was spot-on: "Why did Christ come? Why was He conceived? Why was He born? Why was He crucified? Why did He rise again? Why is He now at the right hand of the Father? The answer to all these questions is, 'In order that He might make worshipers out of rebels.'[5]

Asaph was a worshiper, personally. But *Asaph was also a leader of worshipers.* He was one of three men originally appointed by David to lead others in worship. "David also commanded the chiefs of the Levites to appoint their brothers as the singers who should play loudly on musical instruments, on harps and lyres and cymbals, to raise sounds of joy. So the Levites appointed *Heman* the son of Joel; and of his brothers *Asaph* the son of Berechiah; and of the sons of Merari, their brothers, *Ethan* the son of Kushaiah" (1 Chron. 15:16–17).

Each was a descendant of one of the three sons of Levi.[6] Initially, Asaph served at Heman's right hand and Ethan at his left. Asaph's assignment was to stand before the ark and lead the worshipers into Jerusalem (see 16:5).

This procession "assembled all Israel at Jerusalem" (15:3) and included the sons of Aaron and the Levites (see 15:4). There were over eight hundred worshipers![7] Plus there was David himself, the elders of the people, and the commanders of thousands (see 15:25). Asaph and his brothers took the lead among them (see 15:17). Imagine how this procession must have felt after David's first attempt at bringing up the ark!

Asaph so distinguished himself in leadership that thereafter he lead the worship in Jerusalem where the ark was kept. Once the ark was established in the Tent of Meeting, Heman and Jeduthun were assigned to the Tabernacle in Gibeon (see 1 Chron. 16:39–42), but Asaph became the single leader of worship at the Tent of Meeting before the ark of God in Jerusalem (see 16:4–7).

We know that Asaph was a worshiper and a leader of worshipers. But that doesn't even begin to tell the story. *Asaph was also a leader of worship leaders.*

Asaph's clan continued as leaders of worshipers for generations beyond his own lifetime, serving throughout the history of the Temple built by Solomon. Even after exile in Babylon, to which God had removed His people as discipline for their congenital sin problem, Asaph's descendants returned to be leaders of worship in the rebuilt Temple (see 9:15). Over a hundred of them came back to Jerusalem with Ezra who led a party of God's people back to the Promised Land to restore worship in God's city (see Ezra 2:41; Neh. 7:44). Not long after, the "sons of Asaph" were part of the leadership in another grand procession. This time the descendants of Asaph did not go *into* Jerusalem with the ark, but marched and worshiped *around* Jerusalem atop the newly completed walls (see Neh. 12:31, 35)! They stayed on as regular leaders in worship at the rebuilt Temple (see 11:22; 12:46).[8]

Imagine a single life reproduced over multiple generations to come. Imagine a life lived in such a way that not just the function of it, but the heart of it is carried on for generations to come.

"We've all been carpenters for twelve generations!" some families may claim. "We come from a long line of seamstresses," another may claim. Generation after generation Asaph's family was able to say, "We are all worshipers of God! We all lead worshipers of God! More than that, we're leaders of worship leaders!" This is more than a clan boasting. No, this is much more.

Worship and worship leading characterized Asaph's linage from the time of the beginning of Solomon's Temple construction (962 BC) to the return from exile and securing of the city under Nehemiah (445 BC)—a span of approximately five hundred years.[9]

Few of us can fathom living a life so pointedly, so purposefully, so passionately that half a millennium from now a significant body of our descendants gladly devote themselves to the very thing that we are devoted to, and are leading others to be similarly devoted to that same thing.

It is enough to make us stop and ask, what does Asaph teach us about living a life of worship? Let's ponder together the life of worship captured in this remarkable man.

Demonstrating Living a Life of Worship

What does living a life of worship look like? Despite the passage of thousands of years, Asaph's clear example still shines through to us in the pages of Scripture. For one thing, he reveals that *worship is perpetual*. "So David left Asaph and his brothers there before the ark of the covenant of the LORD to minister *regularly* before the ark as each day required." (1 Chron. 16:37).

Remember, the ark of the covenant was synonymous with the presence of God. Thus daily, regularly, perpetually Asaph appeared in the presence of God with praise. The Hebrew word translated "regularly" means continually or without interruption.[10] It was used to describe the daily burnt offerings, made rhythmically, regularly each morning and evening (see Exod. 29:42). It was used of "the bread of the Presence" that was daily placed and kept before the Lord on the table in the Tabernacle (see 25:30). In fact the word came to describe expressions of worship more generally in the Old Testament:

- "Seek his presence *continually*" (1 Chron. 16:11).
- "His praise shall *continually* be in my mouth" (Ps. 34:1).
- "My praise is *continually* of you" (71:6).
- "I will hope *continually* and will praise you yet more and more" (71:14).
- "May prayer be made for him *continually*" (72:15).
- "Wait *continually* for your God" (Hos. 12:6).

Similarly, the New Testament calls us to a life of perpetual worship: "Through him then let us continually offer up a sacrifice of praise to God" (Heb. 13:15).

With the pressures and demands of life, how do we continually and perpetually worship God? Yes, it means meeting regularly, week-by-week in some cases, for corporate worship with God's people. It certainly intimates that each time we gather we ought to be moved to expressions of worship. It requires that we each daily give expression of our praise to God in our own personal prayer life. And it calls us to pepper our moments and minutes with constant communion and interaction with the Lord throughout the day.

We must be careful that such expressions do not become the mindless repetition of religious clichés but remain active, moment-by-moment engagement with the Lord of life.

The October 1920 edition of *Popular Science* magazine was devoted to the phenomenon of perpetual motion. The cover was a masterful painting by Normal Rockwell. The renowned artist depicted an inventor, clad in his work apron and standing before his workbench. In his left hand, he holds a whirligig contraption—a little like a miniature Ferris wheel—that spins unceasingly and unfailingly without any obvious means of power. His eyes study the contrivance. His expression betrays the cogs and wheels of his mind spinning, trying to make sense of how this device keeps moving. In his right hand, he holds the cap he has snatched from the top of his head. He has freed one finger with which he scratches his head in puzzled amazement.[11]

What a picture of the world observing a life of perpetual worship! How do you keep moving so consistently toward God in praise and adoration? The defeats, dangers, depressions and distractions of life do not impede the motion of your life toward God. You are demanding that "reality" appear for review at God's throne—reverence will define reality!

Those around you are left, hat in hand, scratching their heads as they behold your life. The only plausible explanation is that Someone of infinite glory and grace has captured the wheelhouse of your heart.

Asaph also demonstrates that *worship is proclaimed.* It finds expression and takes form. It comes out from within you and is irrepressible! Worship is a proclamation made *to* God.

For Asaph the proclamation of his worship took three basic forms. It came out in *word.* Asaph was a writer of psalms, and perhaps in the beginning, Asaph received written psalms from David. Perhaps he was asked to set them to music or to oversee their performance (see 1 Chron. 16:7-36), but in time, Asaph apparently began writing his own compositions (see 2 Chron. 29:30). Asaph's worship also came out through *instrument.* Asaph's chosen instrument—are you ready for this?—was the cymbal (see 1 Chron. 16:5)! And, for the glory of the Lord, he played it *loud*! "David also commanded the chiefs of the Levites to appoint their brothers as the singers who should *play loudly* on musical instruments, on harps and lyres and cymbals, to raise sounds of joy. So the Levites appointed. . . Asaph" to play the cymbals (see 15:16–17; 16:5). Is there an echo of Asaph in the last psalm, "Praise him with sounding cymbals; praise him with *loud clashing cymbals*?" (Ps. 150:5).

Certainly Asaph and his brothers had more than a percussion section. They employed stringed instruments such as harps and lyres and wind instruments such as trumpets (see 2 Chron. 5:12).

Finally, to his words and to the instruments, Asaph added his *voice.* He is listed as one of the singers of praise to God (see 1 Chron. 15:19). While the cymbals call for and direct attention, the voice articulates the truth of who God is, what He has done and why He should be praised.

In these three forms of worship, we observe tremendous variety—musical notes given expression through a diversity of instruments and specific words vocalized by numerous worshipers. It reminds us again that everything about everything is about the glory of God and is to lend its borrowed powers to His praise. "Let heaven and earth praise him, the seas and everything that moves in them" (Ps. 69:34).

It is not, of course, that anything and everything goes in worship. It is not to say, *Whatever your expression, let 'er rip!* That's how this whole thing began—with David trying to bring the ark up in a form that seemed best to him. Indeed, in this way a man died.

As David and Uzzah have already shown us, worship is not a do-as-you-please affair. *Worship is what is squeezed out when God moves in.*

Think of it like a child's Play-Doh factory. Did you have one as a child? Into the chamber goes the doughy, soft, clay-like substance. Onto the front the child positions the die with the particular shape she has chosen. Then the pudgy little hand comes down upon the lever, pressing the dough out through the die in the shape of a star, crescent moon, rod, rectangle or whatever other shape she may wish.

When God moves in and rests His weight upon the throne of your heart, the radiance of His presence and the greatness of His Person get squeezed out of our mouths in praises, our minds in thoughts and our hands in service.

Asaph also demonstrates that *worship is prophetic.* "David and the chiefs of the service also set apart for the service the sons of Asaph . . . who *prophesied* with lyres, with harps, and with cymbals" (1 Chron. 25:1). Within this context, "prophecy" is not used in the sense of foretelling the future but as telling the truth about God. Worship is a proclamation made *about* God. Worship makes known something about God. It is a declarative act.

In worship, we are not just speaking *to* God, but *about* God. The apostle Paul commanded, "Let the word of Christ dwell in you richly, teaching and admonishing *one another* in all wisdom, singing psalms and hymns and spiritual songs, with thankfulness in your hearts *to God*" (Col. 3:16). Notice that, simultaneously, we are singing "to God" and speaking about God while "teaching and admonishing one another."

So our corporate singing is "*to* God," but in some sense *for* "one another." It is not a solo endeavor. A worship leader's exhortations to forget everyone around us and to just make it between ourselves and God may be well-intentioned, but can be misguided. God has intentions for those people and He plans to realize some of them through their worship alongside of me. If I forget them entirely I have forgotten something of God's purpose in my worship.

You may have heard a particular song or hymn many times. Perhaps it seems too familiar. Yet by singing it, you are speaking praise to God and building up the people around you. Indeed, there is something irreplaceable about corporate worship, something you cannot duplicate in front of a TV or computer, or via any electronic device. Bits and bytes of digitized images and information can never replace the physical presence and audible sound of other believers joining their voices with yours in prayer and worship to the God who, by His Spirit, has bound you together into a unique people. Proximity to others and proclamation of God go hand in hand.

God did not create us as disembodied voices or cerebral computers. He created us whole—as body, soul and spirit (see 1 Thess. 5:23). As such, He created us in His image, with the capacity for relationship and community. When we dismember and separate out body, soul and spirit, we disconnect ourselves from something vital, deep and spiritual about worship. If the voice is heard, but the body is not present, information may be conveyed, but we need more than information. We are created for connection. There is certain information that is vital—the Bible is filled with it and it alone is the sufficient source of that information. But we receive that most powerfully, process it most thoroughly and integrate it most deeply when we do so together. The Internet and other media serve well as conduits of *information*, but fail to establish the vital, God-intended *connection* that is found in corporate worship.

When we are gathered as God's people, when we are all offering praises in song to God, what are we really saying about God? What is communicated, to God and to those physically around us, if we fold our arms and refuse to sing? Remember, whether we wish to acknowledge it or not, we are saying something both to God and about God! What if I mumble my way through the service, muttering barely audible words under my breath without apparent care? In such a case I may be saying one thing with my whispered words, but quite another with my body language and countenance. Which is my true heart message?

Note again how the chronicler described Asaph: "And Hezekiah the king and the officials commanded the Levites to sing praises to the Lord with the words of David and of *Asaph the seer.* And they sang praises with gladness, and they bowed down and worshiped" (2 Chron. 29:30). The word translated "seer" comes from a root that means "to see." It may imply gazing or looking intently upon something.[12] As I understand it, then, a "seer" was one who set the gaze of his heart upon God and then spoke of what he beheld while in His presence.

Setting the gaze of our hearts upon God has implications for both individual worship and collective worship within our local churches. The quality of your church's corporate worship is directly tied to the quality of week-long individual worship. Failure to seek the presence of God throughout the week will show in your church's corporate worship. If day-by-day we personally worship the Lord, our corporate worship is fueled by the overflow of those encounters.

Corporate worship becomes not about getting recharged before taking on a new week, but about unloading a glad burden of praise that has built up throughout the week to the point we are about to bust. The difference between the two experiences is like the difference between getting an IV and flying a kite.

Asaph's life also reveals that *worship is positional.* Worship demands no particular physical posture. You may kneel, stand or fall prostrate. Your hands may be raised toward heaven or not. Your eyes may gaze upward or they may be cast downward. Your head may be rocked back or bowed toward the floor. The Bible speaks of many postures of worship and prayer. I am not now speaking about any of those.

In saying that worship is positional, I mean worship positions you before God. Worship places you at the throne. Whatever physical posture you may take, worship positions you spiritually before God.

> Seek the LORD and his strength;
> *seek his presence continually!*
> Ascribe to the LORD, O families of the peoples,
> ascribe to the LORD glory and strength!
> Ascribe to the LORD the glory due his name;
> bring an offering and *come before him*!
> Worship the LORD in the splendor of holiness;
> tremble *before him*, all the earth;
> yes, the world is established; it shall never be moved. (1 Chron. 16:11, 28–30)

Do you see the words that David used to frame up the work of worship that he set before Asaph, and which God sets before us? We are to "seek *his presence* continually . . . come *before him* . . . tremble *before him*." Worship is a journey to a place. Not a physical one, but a spiritual one—worship takes us into the very presence of God Himself.

We spend too much time telling God to keep up with us, to walk our road, to come to our house, to be interested in our agenda. We do not spend nearly enough of our energies adjusting our lives to His presence.

Perhaps the most famous of Asaph's songs is Psalm 73. Soon enough we'll look more closely at this ardent prayer-song, this heart cry, but for now simply notice that Asaph begins the prayer by confessing that he is overwhelmed by the apparent blessing of the wicked (see 73:2-15). He is unable to wrap his mind around why God would allow the wicked to prosper (see 73:16). His skewed view of reality was beginning to affect his reverence.

There was no resolution, Asaph admitted, "until I went into the sanctuary of God." It was "then [that] I discerned their end" (73:17).

When Asaph demanded God come down and answer to him about His plans for the wicked, he received no answer, no resolution and no relief. But when Asaph took himself toward God—meeting Him in "the sanctuary of God," coming to Him in worship on His turf—then God resolved the internal struggle that was eating away at him. Reverence has a way of reinterpreting "reality."

Why worship? We worship because everything about everything is about the glory of God. This holds true even in those moments when it seems the wicked prosper. Even in that God has designs for His glory. It is the one who is intent upon glorifying God that enjoys His divine resources. It is the one who is intent upon God's glory that is in line with God's divine purpose in everything.

Quite simply, *worship calibrates us to reality as God has established it.*

Worship, to quote a friend, puts us "under the spout where the glory comes out!"

If you need to clean up, you are not going to take a shower while sitting in your recliner in the family room. You'll have to get up and go into the bathroom, get into the shower and stand under the showerhead! Just as we must be in the proper position to physically cleanse ourselves, we must assume the requisite position as we worship.

Worship positions us before God and puts us in the middle of the action. Worship situates us where grace flows down from His throne in our time of need. Worship puts us where God is moving, speaking, acting, healing and directing. Frankly, only worship puts us in the real world—the world as it actually exists under the direction of a sovereign God. Until we live in this reality, we dance through our days to the rhythm of a piper and a tune that do not in fact exist.

On July 24, 2002, nine men began their workday like any other day. They didn't take an elevator up to their respective offices; rather, they descended some 240 feet below ground at the Quecreek Mine in Somerset, Pennsylvania. These miners were among that rugged stock of men who claw at the belly of the earth while its powerful fist presses down upon them.

Tragically, on this day something went awry. They dug through into the cavity of an old mine shaft, unintentionally opening a flood of fifty million gallons of water into their workspace. Water levels rose rapidly, cutting the men off from escape. The nine found themselves trapped, without resources to free themselves. If they were to live to tell their story, their rescue would have to come from above.

These nine miners instinctively knew survival required repositioning themselves on higher ground. Scrambling to the highest point they could find, they latched themselves together with rope and held on, praying for help to reach them from above.

The rescuers working above also knew what these men knew, so they set about drilling a six-inch shaft to the highest point in the vicinity of where the men had last been working. Miraculously, the trapped men heard the drill break through and soon fresh air was being pumped into their chamber.

Those aboveground labored feverishly to bore a larger, thirty-inch shaft to the men waiting below. Seventy-seven hours after the first drill bit broke through to the men, the last of the nine men appeared through the opening of the 240-foot shaft and embraced life again!

It is known now as the "Quecreek Miracle." The miracle happened because everyone involved knew that life is found in repositioning oneself to high ground. Reflecting on the lessons for worship found in this miracle, Terry Wardle observes,

> Life is about positioning. . . . We are not filled with the Presence because of what we do. No one should say, "I received the infilling of the Spirit because I prayed." No, you prayed and while there the Holy Spirit filled you. You fasted, and while there the Holy Spirit met you. You gathered with other believers in worship and while doing so he empowered you. You positioned. He acted. His action was not driven by your position. Your positioning placed you in the path of God's transforming work.[13]

Worship is for us too, positional. Through worship we move to the high ground of God's presence where we find Him reciprocating our approach and drawing near to us (see James 4:8).

We are all worshipers by default—blind idolaters to a man. No one begins in a position of right worship. We must move; all the adjustments are on our side. We must reposition ourselves before God because He has priority. He is the touchstone. God is the standard. God represents perfect pitch and He is the tuning fork. We must adjust to Him, not He to us.

So, as we begin this journey, the message is pretty simple: we can't stay where we are and worship God. If Asaph teaches us anything, it is that a life lived as worship is *a life constantly adjusting to God*. The chapters ahead are going to reveal the adjustments necessary to reposition ourselves to God, the adjustments required to live *life as worship*.

Sound a bit threatening? Know that God's intent is to rescue us from merely passing time and to move us into living *life as worship*. In worship, we tap into the eternal, transcending the bounds of time, space and circumstance. Worship launches us into the unbounded and infinite.

Think of the amazing legacy of Asaph—one man utterly committed to the glory of God. Remember this: Enduring influence with men is achieved through temporal adjustments to God. Lasting influence with mankind is achieved through personal adjustments to God.

The Ways of Worship

- The first and most basic adjustment we must make is to relationship with God. The Father made this possible through His Son Jesus Christ. He paid the penalty of our sins, which is separation from God through death (see Rom. 6:23). Jesus did this on the cross and then rose again to indestructible life. Through repentance (adjusting our life from self-reliance and self-righteousness to Christ-reliance and God-provided righteousness in Jesus) and faith we enter a living relationship with God.
- Rely on God. Turn from reliance upon yourself to reliance upon Christ for relationship to God.
- Set aside an unhurried period of solitude to express your repentance and faith in Christ through prayer. With specific words renounce any reliance upon yourself, your works and your righteousness, establishing yourself in faith upon Christ alone. End with prayers of gratitude for God's free gift of eternal life through faith in Christ (see Rom. 6:23).

2

Living a Life of Thankfulness

Psalm 50

"Art, like morality," asserted G.K. Chesterton, "consists of drawing the line somewhere."[1]

With both artistic intent and moral impulse the Holy Spirit put pen to paper and drew the line somewhere. In this case that "somewhere" is found in the psalms of Asaph. There are twelve such psalms. They are, if you will, twelve lines drawn on the pages of Holy Scripture. Just twelve lines. Twelve lines, however, which sketch the profile of *life as worship*. The full portrait would take many more lines, but these twelve set before us a clear profile of life as worship.

The first psalm-stroke draws a line for thankfulness. It is no great shock that gratitude is essential to a life of worship. What may be unexpected, however, is just how the psalmist depicts the need for thanksgiving.

Surprisingly, Asaph takes our hand and leads us, not to the sanctuary, but to a courtroom. A courtroom rarely lends itself to thoughts of thankfulness, unless you are in the gal-ley, grateful not to be the defendant. Yet in this psalm, we are defendants and the only gratitude we "can imagine would come with the announcement of a "not guilty". Yet the psalm tells us precisely the opposite—that we are indeed guilty of all charges, convicted of our crime.

Here in the cold, legal world of the courtroom, how then do we find our way to thanksgiving?

Shhh! We'll get there soon enough, but for now, the case begins . . .

All rise for the honorable John Doe!

Sessions in our modern day courtrooms begin like this, though the name of the judge will change from courtroom to courtroom. But in all cases the bailiff lifts his voice, commanding those in attendance to rise because the judge is about to enter the courtroom. Everyone and everything adjusts to the presence of the judge. Someone of great authority is about to take his place.

The opening of Psalm 50 is no different.

The Court is Convened

Behold, the Judge enters His courtroom!

> 1 The Mighty One, God the LORD,
> speaks and summons the earth
> from the rising of the sun to its setting.

It takes no special insight to see *this Judge is awesome!* He is the "Mighty One"—the Hebrew *El* emphasizing God's power. He is the Majestic One—the Hebrew *Elohim* ("God") denoting Him as creator God. He is the Merciful One—*Yahweh* ("LORD") denoting Him as the covenant-making, covenant-keeping God.[2]

These three divine names appear together in only one other place in the Old Testament. And there they were taken up with the greatest solemnity as the people of the tribes of Reuben, Gad and the half-tribe of Manasseh sought to deny the charge of treachery made by their fellow Israelites: "The Mighty One, God, the LORD! The Mighty One, God, the LORD! He knows; and let Israel itself know! If it was in rebellion or in breach of faith against the LORD, do not spare us today" (Josh. 22:22).

Clearly, something dreadfully serious is underway.

This Judge is beautiful!

> 2 Out of Zion, the perfection of beauty,
> God shines forth.

He had once shone out from Mount Sinai, with terrifying displays of power, as He delivered His Law to Moses. But now it is not from Sinai nor for the delivery of the Law, but from Mount Zion—Jerusalem—that God shines forth. It is not now for the delivery of the Law, but for judgment over failure to keep that Law that God beams forth His glory and convenes His court.

This Judge is terrifying!

> 3 Our God comes; he does not keep silence;
> before him is a devouring fire,
> around him a mighty tempest.

This sounds very much like the description of God coming to Mount Sinai.

> On the morning of the third day there were thunders and lightnings and a thick cloud on the mountain and a very loud trumpet blast, so that all the people in the camp trembled. Then Moses brought the people out of the camp to meet God, and they took their stand at the foot of the mountain. Now Mount Sinai was wrapped in smoke because the LORD had descended on it in fire. The smoke of it went up like the smoke of a kiln, and the whole mountain trembled greatly.

> And as the sound of the trumpet grew louder and louder, Moses spoke, and God answered him in thunder. (Exod. 19:16–19; see Heb. 12:18–24)

This Judge comes with "a mighty tempest"—no soothing rainstorm, but one of the infamous wind storms that blew in from the eastern desert. With vacuous, scorching heat the arid winds sucked the animating juices from every living thing on the face of the earth. In mere hours, it made a desolate waste of a fertile plain. God enters with blistering holiness into His courtroom.

It may not seem we're getting any closer to thankfulness. In fact gratitude may seem to be slipping away, but let's keep an eye on the picture God is painting.

The Judge is not alone in His courtroom. Witnesses have been beckoned. The Judge "summons the earth from the rising of the sun to its setting" (Ps. 50:1). This is not a reference to time, from sunup to sundown, nor is it a reference to geography, from east to west. Rather it is a summons to all the peoples of the earth who live out their lives under that sun and in all those geographical places over which it passes. All the peoples of the earth are beckoned, not as plaintiffs, but as witnesses. Added to these witnesses are "the heavens above and . . . the earth" (50:4). Therefore all of creation, above our heads and below our feet, is called upon to bear witness to the proceedings about to take place.

Like every courtroom, the bailiff is present. He lifts his voice and cries:

> 6 The heavens declare his righteousness,
> for God himself is judge! Selah

Everything above our heads cries out, *This Judge is just!*

Here we encounter the mysterious "*Selah*" (Ps. 50:6). Scholars are not able with certainty to tell us just what this word intends. Most agree, however, that it was probably a musical notation of some kind, perhaps exhorting the singer-prayer to stop, to take a momentary pause, to be silent and to reflect upon what has just been said.

Indeed, considering before whom we now stand and bearing in mind the weightiness of the matters to be brought into judgment, a moment of intentional, quiet reflection is wise. The Bible often calls us to such stillness and reflection:

- "But the Lord is in his holy temple; let all the earth keep silence before him" (Hab. 2:20).
- "Be silent, all flesh, before the Lord, for he has roused himself from his holy dwelling" (Zech. 2:13).
- "Cease striving and know that I am God; I will be exalted among the nations, I will be exalted in the earth" (Ps. 46:10, NASB).
- "When the Lamb opened the seventh seal, there was silence in heaven for about half an hour" (Rev. 8:1).

Now, drawing a fresh breath and taking a fresh accounting of our surroundings, note that the defendants have also entered the courtroom. Who are these that stand on trial? "He calls to the heavens above and to the earth, that he may judge *his people*" (Ps. 50:4). They are further designated as "my faithful ones" , those who have "made a covenant with me by sacrifice" (50:5). God calls them "my people," "Israel" (50:7).

Deep breath. Emerging feelings of relief!

Okay, so far, so good. Maybe this isn't as bad as it appeared at first. But with relentless pace the description continues. These same people are now called, "the wicked" (Ps. 50:16). They are the very ones "who forget God" (50:22). The Judge, from His lofty vantage point, locks eyes with them and reminds them, "I am God, your God" (50:7). Here is again an echo, reverberating down the slopes of Sinai. For this is how God began His address to the people before delivering the Ten Commandments: "I am the LORD your God" (Exod. 20:2).

Reality is beginning to settle in. The truth is starting to emerge: God is indicting those who call themselves His people! Indeed, "It is time for judgment to begin at the household of God" (1 Pet. 4:17).

By now you may be asking, *Why are we here?*

It is a fair question. Notice what happens next.

The Charges are Brought

We are here because formal charges have been filed against we who identify ourselves as God's people. Two indictments are brought against us.[3] The first: *religious formalism*. Listen carefully.

> 7 Hear, O my people, and I will speak;
> O Israel, I will testify against you.
> I am God, your God.
>
> 8 Not for your sacrifices do I rebuke you;
> your burnt offerings are continually before me.
>
> 9 I will not accept a bull from your house
> or goats from your folds.
>
> 10 For every beast of the forest is mine,
> the cattle on a thousand hills.
>
> 11 I know all the birds of the hills,
> and all that moves in the field is mine.
>
> 12 If I were hungry, I would not tell you,
> for the world and its fullness are mine.

13 Do I eat the flesh of bulls
or drink the blood of goats?

When, you may wonder aloud, *did I do this?*

It was not wrong that they brought sacrifices, for that's what God had outlined. It was that they brought *only* their sacrifices. They brought sacrifices to God without also bringing an accompanying heart of worship. God reminds us, "I don't need your sacrifices!" We worship not to fill a deficiency within God, not because of any need within Him. Pagan peoples sometimes thought of their gods as "eating" the sacrifices they brought to their altars (see Ps. 50:12–13).[4] "Where are their gods . . . who ate the fat of their sacrifices and drank the wine of their drink offering?" (Deut. 32:37–38).

But God is not like any other god. In fact there are no other gods (see 1 Cor. 8:4). God alone is God! Yet these, "His people," were treating Him just as the pagans approached their gods. These people were faithful in their religious routines, but rote in that faithfulness. They were habitual in their worship, but their worship was merely habit and not from the heart. They worshiped outwardly, but not inwardly. They performed the religious rituals, but experienced no spiritual reality. They possessed no real relationship with God.

We might say they came to "church." They regularly went to "worship." They were in "the service" each week—praying the prayers, singing the songs, giving their gifts, opening their Bibles, taking notes during the sermon, serving in a ministry, polishing their Sunday school attendance awards, keeping the code, doing the deeds, jumping the religious hoops, doing the church-thing. They had convinced themselves that they were living a life of worship.

But something is wrong with this picture. Something is missing. It has all become rote—a mere habit, routine. We have failed to understand that "God is spirit, and those who worship him must worship in spirit and truth" (John 4:24).

Hard to hear as this is, there is also a second charge: *religious hypocrisy.*

> 16 But to the wicked God says:
> "What right have you to recite my statutes
> or take my covenant on your lips?
>
> 17 For you hate discipline,
> and you cast my words behind you."

They too did "the church-thing." God could rightly assert, You "recite my statutes." Trouble was, God could also accurately report "You cast my words behind you." Then, as if putting his finger upon the stone tablets of God's Law, the psalmist recounts their lawlessness even as they convince themselves they are worshipers of the true God.

"If you see a thief, you are pleased with him" (Ps. 50:18). Let's see, that's the eighth commandment. They pilfered, pinched and pocketed things that were not theirs.

"And you keep company with adulterers" (50:18). Seventh commandment? *Check!*

> 19 "You give your mouth free rein for evil,
> and your tongue frames deceit.
>
> 20 You sit and speak against your brother;
> you slander your own mother's son."

That would be the ninth commandment: "You shall not bear false witness against your neighbor" (Exod. 20:16).

When do I do that?

How about when you call, text or e-mail someone? How about via whatever social media forum you frequent these days? What about when you stop them at church and ask, "What do you think of ________?" and then sweetly sit in the service and piously add your "amen" to the end of the prayers and lift your voice in songs.

Such folk are regularly in attendance at "worship," but are only "the alleged people of God."[5] We are more than capable of saying the right things in the service and then living as we see fit.

The Error is Exposed

Our failure stems from two fatal misinterpretations regarding the very God we claim to worship. The Judge clears His voice and announces: "Now I rebuke you and lay the charge before you" (Ps. 50:21).

The first error involves *a misinterpretation of God's silences.* "These things you have done, and I have been silent" (50:21). True, in the past God had been silent, but now He is speaking. It has been said that "silence is a text easy to misread."[6] The people of God had interpreted His silence as approval.

Could it be time to rethink the silences of God in your life?

Consider the case of Frank and Sally.[7] It has been less than twelve months since their wedding day. Sally is in the kitchen working on dinner; Frank is in the living room doing something else. Through the open doorway Sally is talking a steady stream—complaining about this situation, talking about that person, griping about something else. Likely she wasn't even aware of the nature of her discourse. Through all this Frank has remained silent, something Sally interprets as approval, agreement, permission to continue. And all is well until Frank finally breaks the silence with a stern and serious tone, "Sally, I'm getting angry!"

Never assume silence equals approval.

A second error involves *a misinterpretation of God's character.*

21 you thought that I was one like yourself.
But now I rebuke you and lay the charge before you.

22 Mark this, then, you who forget God,
lest I tear you apart, and there be none to deliver!

They did what we've been guilty of countless times. In their default thinking patterns, they reversed the facts—making God in their own image, rather than seeing themselves as made in His image. It is no minor miscalculation. This is pagan reasoning. Biblical commentator John Phillips writes, "The ancient Greeks were guilty of this. They peopled Mount Olympus with gods made in the image and likeness of men. They projected into infinity the lines of their own fallen natures and invented gods who were just larger editions of themselves."[8]

Pagans make their gods by drawing lines from man upward. The gods are like us, only bigger, faster, stronger.

The film *The Avengers* is a case in point. Thor, the god of thunder, is like us only stronger (and with a bigger hammer!). Captain America is just how we'd like to picture ourselves, only stronger, wiser and nobler. The Hulk too is like us, only not in entirely positive ways. He is angry, like us . . . but unlike us, in a kind of loveable way.

At one point in the film, the Hulk storms through a window, throwing the evil villain Loki against a wall. Loki declares, "I am a god, you dull creature! I will not be bullied by a . . ." His pronouncement is cut short when the Hulk takes up Loki by the legs and, before he can finish speaking, repeatedly slams him to the ground. Having pulverized the wannabe god, the Hulk stomps sullenly away.

Loki, stunned and motionless upon the ground, can only emit a high, shrill moan, disbelieving what has just happened.

The Hulk, stomping off to pitch the battle elsewhere, is heard to murmur under his breath, "Puny god."[9]

The call of the Bible is to measure man by God, not God by man. We rightly measure from God down to ourselves, when looking to identify reality. God is holy—other—unlike anything we know. Neither He nor His ways can be discerned by lines of comparison. We are created. We are able to understand something about ourselves by looking at God. We are on dangerous ground, however, when we seek to understand God by looking at ourselves. A.W. Tozer was correct when he said, "What comes into our minds when we think about God is the most important thing about us."[10]

The Verdict is Rendered

Finally, the Judge clears His throat and lifts His voice. His verdict will lay down the starting line for true worship.

The courtroom falls silent. Heaven and earth lean toward His throne. Angels, ancients, our contemporaries and the generations yet to come all cup their ears, knowing that what comes next is a game changer. All eternity hangs upon the Judge's next words. God renders the verdict—a three-pronged exposition of the beginning point of all worship—one truth telescoping into the next.

Truth 1: *True worship begins with thankfulness.*

"Offer to God a sacrifice of thanksgiving" (Ps. 50:14). The marginal reading in the English Standard Version says, "Make thanksgiving your sacrifice." The point echoes down through the psalm, "This one who offers thanksgiving as his sacrifices glorifies me" (Ps. 50:23). This is all about our basic orientation in worship. Worship says not, "I've got something to earn," or

"I've got something to do," or "I've got something to prove." Genuine worship begins with the realization, "I've received something I don't deserve!"

Truth 2: *Thankfulness begins with grace.*

Thankfulness arises from the awareness that you enjoy something you don't deserve. Gratitude looks upon a sunset and knows it didn't make it. A thankful man gazes upon his wife and reasons, "I don't deserve a woman like her!" Appreciation stares at the gift being extended, reaches out its arms and says, "I couldn't have expected this and I certainly don't deserve it!"

Now consider this from our privileged vantage point on this side of the cross and empty tomb. "For the grace of God has appeared, bringing salvation for all people" (Titus 2:11). In the person of Jesus Christ, God Himself has descended from heaven to rescue you from all that binds you, all that threatens you, all that would damn you. Jesus is the "grace of God" held out to you as the gospel-gift!

Little wonder Paul shouted with his pen, "Thanks be to God for his inexpressible gift!" (2 Cor. 9:15).

An authentic response to that true grace always shows up in specific acts of obedience. Thus the psalmist calls out, "perform your vows to the Most High" (Ps. 50:14). The true worshiper is "one who orders his way rightly" (50:23).

Don't lose focus now! Keep following the telescoping logic.

True worship begins with thankfulness. Thankfulness begins with grace. And now observe:

Truth 3: *Grace always begins with God.*

God, the Judge, thus draws the line somewhere. And it is not where this courtroom drama seemed to be leading us, is it? The divine line in the sand is not a stroke of judgment, but of grace.

John put it most eloquently: "For God so loved the world, that he gave his only Son, that whoever believes in him should not perish but have eternal life" (John 3:16). God is always the initiator. Grace begins with God. We are ever in the position of responders.

Have you crossed that line? Responded to God's grace? To Jesus? To His sufferings and death in your place? To the empty tomb? To the enthroned Christ, exalted at the Father's right hand? To life as He governs it and hands it to you each day?

Earlier we began by asking the question, *Lord, what must change for me to live a life of worship?* The answer is simply, my perception of God, of me, of my life. Indeed, of worship itself. Worship begins in realizing that all of life is a response, a response to grace extended and undeserved.

Worship in Action

- Set aside some unhurried time with God. Find a place where you will not be interrupted and where you may be audible with your prayers.
- Ask God to reveal to you the ways you have overlooked His grace. Write them down. Make a list. Linger patiently and allow God to lay bare all He wishes to show you.
- Determine to spend the next fifteen minutes in a continuous, steady stream of thanksgiving to God. No asking. No demanding. No seeking. No petitions, intercessions or requests. Pure gratitude—for the little and the big, the previously-thought-of and the never-thought-of, for the life-changing and the hardly-noticed. "Offer to God a sacrifice of thanksgiving" (Ps. 50:14).
- Conclude your season of worship by sitting in silence before the Lord, quietly basking in the joy of being His and enjoying His goodness.

3

Living a Life of Perspective

Psalm 73

Worship can't wait for ideal conditions, because such conditions do not yet exist.

God has designed an eternity of worship to take place in ideal conditions, but in this world our worship is always folded into the fabric of the chaos that lies across life on this temporal plane. This is precisely why, if we are to live life as worship, we must gain new perspective. But such perspective comes at a steep price. Let's observe the perspective shift in the following scenario.

Mom, Dad, can I borrow the car?

Why? What do you have planned?

An evening with friends.

After a moment of reflection, you hand her the keys.

But now it is two hours past her curfew. She hasn't been answering her cell phone. Frantic, wild, erratic thoughts refuse to be wrestled into submission to your faith.

Then the door flies open. In she walks, trembling and clearly shaken. She throws herself into the chair opposite you and exhales: *I've got a story to tell you! But first let me say that the car is fine, I'm fine, no one else is hurt and you won't be getting a call from the police.*

Though you don't yet know the whole story, her words give you the confidence to rethink the past several hours from a perspective your frantic emotions denied just moments ago. Clearly, not all the news will be welcome, but knowing the outcome offers nerves the reprieve necessary to hear your daughter out.

This was precisely Asaph's strategy as he penned Psalm 73. He says, in essence, "I've been through a terrible crisis of faith. I'm going to recount it for you. But first let me tell you the outcome. Then I'll tell you the story of my trauma."

First, the outcome. Asaph's conclusion:

> 1 Truly God is good to Israel,
> to those who are pure in heart.

Easy to say! Much harder to live.

Dr. E.V. Hill, the renowned preacher from East Los Angeles, used to tell the story of a beloved deacon who had served long and faithfully in the church. Each Sunday morning he would greet Dr. Hill, "Brother Pastor, the Lord am good." To which Dr. Hill would always respond, "Brother Deacon, the Lord *is* good." And the reply was always the same, "Yes he am!"[1]

I remember well one of my professors Dr. Harold Burchett, many years ago now, looking us young, wannabe pastors in the eye and instructing us that sometimes the best you can do for someone mired in deep trauma is to get them to confess honestly in prayer: "You are good, and what you do is good" (Ps. 119:68, NIV).

The person won't yet feel it. It won't yet resonate within her soul. But by faith, with a will resolutely set to believe God's Word in spite of what seems to be temporal evidence to the contrary, she can declare, "You are good, and what you do is good." She can say with that faithful deacon, "the Lord *am* good." Yes, the Lord *is* good—right now, right here, in my circumstances, in His dealings with me, even if I don't see, understand or feel it as deeply as I'd like at this precise moment.

That is an act of determined worship.

Asaph had known the trauma, but now he has come out on the other side. He can, with a glad and convinced heart, say, "Truly God is good to Israel"!

Having established this as the settled conviction of his heart, Asaph says, "Buckle up and let me tell you the story of how I arrived at this conclusion."

I Experienced a Crisis: It Pays to Be Wicked!

Asaph, like so many of us, came to a moment of crisis, a turning point, a pivot, an implosion, a meltdown, a fork in the road. For some reason that he probably didn't entirely understand himself, Asaph cut the engine that had powered him forward in sacred fervor for all these years. Like a powerful wake, all his religious zeal caught up to him, washing up under him. Dead in the water. It is eerie. In the awkward quietness, doubts leap from the heart.

Asaph confessed, "I almost lost my faith."

> 2 But as for me, my feet had almost stumbled,
> my steps had nearly slipped.

"In that moment, my faith had all the stability of one standing on a rain-slicked mountain of mud in bare feet!"

> 3 For I was envious of the arrogant
> when I saw the prosperity[2] of the wicked.

"I've got to tell you," Asaph admits, "I looked down from my fragile perch on the muddy slope of faith and those in the valley below looked pretty happy, contented and well-off. Look at the evidence! Gaze down into the valley with me! Don't they all enjoy good health?"

> 4 For they have no pangs until death;
> their bodies are fat and sleek.

To us "fat" sounds unflattering and unattractive. To the people of Asaph's day, "fat" advertised prosperity, wealth and success. It is the same today in many developing nations. In lands where life is a hand-to-mouth affair, where one summer of drought can wipe out entire people groups, to be "fat" is a sign of having risen above that kind of tenuous existence. We might say, "They live as they want, haven't been to the doctor in years and are the picture of health."

Not only this, they enjoy a trouble-free life!

> 5 They are not in trouble as others are;
> they are not stricken like the rest of mankind.

We chime in with Asaph and in our day wonder: *Don't they seem to live charmed lives? They don't drive cars that die in the middle of a busy intersection! They don't lose their jobs! Their homes never go into foreclosure. Their water heaters don't need replacing just after the washer needed replacing, which came right after the drains backed up sewage in the basement, right after the air-conditioning went on the fritz. They seem to pass through life on a hovercraft twelve inches above all the troubles of the common person!*

What's more, they seem to enjoy some kind of moral indemnity.

6 Therefore pride is their necklace; [They wear arrogance like jewelry!]
violence covers them as a garment. [They bully and oppress whom they like!]

7 Their eyes swell out through fatness;
Their hearts overflow with follies.

Again we protest: *God appears either not to notice or not to care. It seems they have a laminated, lifetime "get-out-of-jail-free" card!*

In all this they mock God, and there are no repercussions.

8 They scoff and speak with malice;
loftily they threaten oppression.

9 They set their mouths against the heavens,
and their tongue struts through the earth.

And what are God's people to conclude?

10 Therefore his people turn back to them,
and find no fault in them.

11 And they say, "How can God know?
Is there knowledge in the Most High?"[3]

12 Behold,[4] these are the wicked;
always at ease, they increase in riches.

"Here," confides Asaph, "was my conclusion at the time."

13 All in vain have I kept my heart clean
and washed my hands in innocence.

14 For all the day long I have been stricken
and rebuked every morning.

"I'm telling you, it doesn't pay to honor God. God's governing of His universe is in moral deficit. Is it that God doesn't know or that He doesn't care? I honestly don't know, but either way it doesn't much change things where I live. I have been snookered, hoodwinked, deceived—by God Himself."

Thus Asaph pauses, chest heaving in moral outrage and exhaustion. His eyes lock on yours.

I told you this would be unsettling.

Or it may be reassuring in some strange way. Maybe because it's where you find yourself at the moment.

You're on the steep mountain of faith, it's raining hard, the ground beneath your feet is turning to grease—and your bare feet are starting to slip.

And, honestly, it's got you scared.

I Turned a Corner: It Pays to Worship!

"Yet somehow I knew this wasn't right."

> 15 If I had said, "I will speak thus,"
> I would have betrayed the generation of your children.

"I felt it with every fiber of my being, but I just couldn't bring myself to articulate those doubt-filled feelings in audible words."

Asaph, perhaps like you, is trying to decide whether to express the crisis that is brewing inside him. He is a worshiper of God. He is a leader of worshipers. He is a leader of worship leaders. How could he possibly admit what was really in his heart?

It has been largely an internal struggle until now. Hidden thoughts. Inner calculations. Unexpressed questions. Masked outrage. Muted anger. A silent sense of injustice.

Unexpressed, these feelings fester. In the closed system of inward, unexpressed thoughts the bacteria of doubt begins feeding on the flesh of faith. Before long you're about to burst.

But something tells you that despite what seems to be overwhelming evidence to the contrary and the witness of your heart, there is something not quite right about your conclusions.

So far none of this has made its way to your lips during worship, but it surely has been in your head as you have bowed before God in prayer.

"Yet I still couldn't get my head around this."

> 16 But when I thought how to understand this,
> it seemed to me a wearisome task.

It all was like an unsolvable Rubik's Cube.

Not long ago, a German high school student solved a three hundred-year-old math problem which had first been proposed by Sir Isaac Newton.[5] Think about this: For thirty decades the brightest minds on the planet played with this conundrum and couldn't make heads or tails of it. But then, suddenly, one high school student saw it!

Asaph, too, had his *aha* moment.

And, I pray, it will happen for you.

"Then I saw it!" Asaph can barely contain himself. "Light came! And it arrived *while I was worshiping!*"

Asaph plied the answers with a weary mind. This went on "until I went into the sanctuary of God." There in the presence of God, with his heart beholding again the glory of God, Asaph admitted, "*then* I discerned their end" (Ps. 73:17).

By "the sanctuary of God" Asaph undoubtedly meant the temple in Jerusalem. That's where they went to worship God, to hear His Word and to pray. In broad strokes, it was perhaps a bit like what we do when we gather with other believers today. But it wasn't so much about the *place* he went to worship. It was about the *person* he sought in worship. Asaph sought to put God front and center. When we worship God for who He is, life and circumstances find their appropriate place.

It is like a mariner adrift in an angry sea for weeks—no sun by day, no moon or stars by night. Only—as far as the eye can see in every direction —a wild, tossing sea sealed over by leaden skies. The mariner wonders, *Where am I? What is happening to me? Which direction am I going? What will become of me?*

Then, in the dark watches of a black night, clouds part and skies open. There it is! The northern star! Sextant in hand, a reading is taken. Suddenly his location is discerned, his direction is determined. Hope is reborn!

Worship is the land of light, illumination, perspective. "For with you is the fountain of life; in your light do we see light" (Ps. 36:9).

I Reached a Conclusion: It Pays to Wait!

In that moment Asaph exclaimed, "I was able to discern the end that awaits the wicked!" As author Donald Williams puts it, "When we know how the novel ends, we understand the plot. Contradictory clues now make sense."[6]

> 18 Truly you set them in slippery places;
> you make them fall to ruin.
>
> 19 How they are destroyed in a moment,
> swept away utterly by terrors!
>
> 20 Like a dream when one awakes,
> O Lord, when you rouse yourself, you despise
> them as phantoms.

Before he gave himself to renewed worship and when his mind still reeled with distorted thinking, Asaph himself stood on slippery ground.

> 2 But as for me, my feet had almost stumbled,
> my steps had nearly slipped.

But now he sees. What he observes is that it is actually the feet of the godless that slip. Their triumph was only an apparent success, and their security was only an illusory sanctuary. Their serenity was only a phantom peace.

Similar to well-known Looney Tunes character Wile E. Coyote chasing Roadrunner, the wicked inevitably find themselves standing in midair, having run off some cliff in their headlong, but godless, pursuit. Their life in this world—with all its apparent success and engendering all their pride—consists only of that split second of hang time before their unavoidable descent to ruin begins.

The renowned British journalist Malcolm Muggeridge late in life became an ardent defender of the Christian faith. He famously noted:

> We look back upon history, and what do we see? Empires rising and falling, revolutions and counterrevolutions, wealth accumulated and wealth disbursed. Shakespeare has written of the rise and fall of great ones, that ebb and flow with the moon.
>
> I look back upon my own fellow countrymen, once upon a time dominating a quarter of the world, most of them convinced, in the words of what is still a popular song, that "the God who made them mighty, shall make them mightier yet."
>
> I've heard a crazed, cracked Austrian announce to the world the establishment of a Reich that would last a thousand years.

> I have seen an Italian clown say he was going to stop and restart the calendar with his own ascension to power. I've heard a murderous Georgian brigand in the Kremlin, acclaimed by the intellectual elite of the world as being wiser than Solomon, more humane than Marcus Aurelius, more enlightened than Ashoka.
>
> I have seen America wealthier and, in terms of military weaponry, more powerful than the rest of the world put together—so that had the American people so desired, they could have outdone a Caesar or an Alexander in the range and scale of their conquests.
>
> All in one lifetime, all in one lifetime, all gone! Gone with the wind!
>
> England, now part of a tiny island off the coast of Europe, threatened with dismemberment and even bankruptcy. Hitler and Mussolini dead, remembered only in infamy. Stalin a forbidden name in the regime he helped found and dominate for some three decades. America haunted by fears of running out of those precious fluids that keeps their motorways roaring, and the smog settling, with troubled memories of a disastrous campaign in Vietnam, and the victories of the Don Quixote's of the media as they charged the windmills of Watergate.
>
> All in one lifetime, all in one lifetime, all gone! Gone with the wind![7]

The same will be true one day for the power-hungry, praise-seeking, applause-drunk leaders of our own age. Their names will be added to the sad memorial celebrating the temporal nature of earthbound vision and conquests. They too, for all their apparent triumph in this life, will have earned the epitaph "Gone with the wind!"

Not only did Asaph discern the damnable end toward which the wicked rush, but he could say, "I was able to discern the joys of worship." The ancient worshiper tells us those joys are at least four in number.

First, worship affords us the joy of *understanding from God.*

> 21 When my soul was embittered,
> when I was pricked in heart,
>
> 22 I was brutish and ignorant;
> I was like a beast toward you.

The clear implication is that now, having sincerely worshiped in God's presence: "I am no longer brutish and ignorant like a beast."

Beasts pass their days moving through God's world on the basis of instinct, not understanding. It is in worship that insight and understanding are restored to us. Note carefully how Asaph's perspective changed as the psalm progresses.

The first third of the psalm is dominated by the words "they," "their" and "these"—referring to the wicked—(73:2–12). He can't get his eyes off of the apparent success of those who seem to flout God and yet find all good things.

The middle of the psalm is dominated by "I," "me" and "my" and refers to Asaph himself (73:13–17). Asaph's eyes soon enough return home to take stock of what his devout worship of God has gained—or apparently failed to gain—him. The man of God finds himself in spiritual crisis.

But in time, through disciplined and sustained worship, the eyes of his heart are reestablished, not upon the wicked, nor upon himself, but upon God ("you," 73:18–22). At that intersection of God ("you") and His worshiper ("me"), divine insight is granted (73:23–26).

In the end, all three come together within the panorama of God-given understanding. The wicked: "Those who are far from you shall perish." God: "You put an end to everyone who is unfaithful to you" (Ps. 73:27). The true worshiper of God: "But for me it is good to be near God; I have made the Lord God my refuge, that I may tell of all your works" (73:28).[8]

Second, worship affords us the joy of *fellowship with God.* "Nevertheless, I am continually with you" (73:23).

Despite my doubts and my near fall from faith, I awake from the darkness of my doubt and discover that, by God's grace, I am still with him!

Notice the psalmist does not say "you are still with me," as if God adjusts His schedule and reworks His day to chase after us in our far flung escapades. No, it tells us that in our benighted crisis of faith God keeps us with Him, and He does so by means of the discipline of worship.

But how?

The simplicity is breathtaking:

"You hold my right hand" (73:23).

All this time that I've been blaming God for being distant and uncaring, He has been right here, holding my hand! When standing on that rain-slicked, mud-greased slope of faith, nearly ready to topple from the battering winds of doubt, God Himself was holding me by the hand and steadying me there.

Third, worship affords us the joy of *counsel from God.*

> 24 You guide me with your counsel,
> and afterward you will receive me to glory.

When we stop complaining and begin listening carefully to God's Word, we find the light we need for the next step along life's path. And though that light doesn't always shine very far down the path, the next step it illumines takes us to the place where we see enough light for another step and, in time, another, and, as it is required, yet another. One step at a time that light always leads us *home*—to the presence of God, to the safety of His will, to the place where His glory shines.

Finally, worship affords us the joy of *fresh satisfaction in God.*

> 25 Whom have I in heaven but you?
> And there is nothing on earth that I desire
> besides you.

I have come to see that I have been miscalculating who is the rich one around here!

> 26 My flesh and my heart may fail,
> but God is the strength of my heart.

Literally, God is "the rock of my heart." God alone takes me off the slippery slopes of doubt and plants my feet on a high, steady, stable rock. God alone is "my portion forever" (Ps. 73:26). This is inheritance talk. I am suddenly a rich man, and by no doing of my own!

The worshiper can pray, *God, I have come to see that there are many things in this life that I may not get to enjoy. Honestly, that makes me a little sad at times, but I've resolved in my heart that You are my inheritance. You are what I get out of this deal. In this life and in even greater fullness in the next, You are my portion. You are my inheritance and in You I am rich. You are more than sufficient for my every need! You are more than I could ever have expected and You are the joy of my heart.*

And so we and Asaph can say together, *Here is my final answer . . .*

> 27 For behold, those who are far from you shall perish;
> you put an end to everyone who is unfaithful to you.

> 28 But for me it is good to be near God;
> I have made the Lord GOD my refuge,
> that I may tell of all your works.

Asaph and all who join him in the perspective which God grants through persistent, resolute worship can reflect, *And thus, I end where I began . . .*

> 1 Truly God is *good* to Israel,
> to those who are pure in heart . . .
>
> 28 But for me it is *good* to be near God;
> I have made the Lord GOD my refuge,
> that I may tell of all your works.

Is it *easy* to be near God, to know His presence, to discern His ways? No, definitely not. But is it *good*? Oh yes, absolutely! His presence is worth everything the discipline of worship demands. The key that unlocks this kind of perspective is the presence of God. And the presence of God is only experienced in worship. It is only in God's presence that we are able rightly to perceive the finish line of the race we are all running. Accurately identifying the finish line and running *through* it is essential—whether in track and field or in our journey with God.

When an adolescent, I was a track athlete. But our track team was made up of numbers that were disproportionately small even for our tiny town. A number of our guys were somewhat accomplished, and in fact we were often in second or third place as a team after the field events and the sprints. But when it came time for the relays, we just didn't have the numbers to compete with the larger schools. One can only run so many races in one night. Inevitably, as the evening wore on toward the meet's conclusion, we slipped further and further down the team standings.

One spring day, our coach decided he would pull some of our best runners from their individual races and piece together a quartet of runners for the medley relay, just to see what would happen. He pulled our best sprinters from their events, but when it came to the closing half-mile leg of the relay, he chose our second-best runner. After the first three of us had completed our legs of the race and I had handed the baton to our last runner, we had a commanding lead. Over the first of his two laps our half-miler held the ground pretty well, but in that final lap he began to swoon. In the closing yards, he gave up the lead to more than one runner. Frustrated to have lost the lead handed to him, as he crossed the finish line, he threw the baton down the track in a rage. And with that, the race officials disqualified our relay team and, instead of collecting at least a few points, we were awarded a disqualification.

I doubt Asaph ran track. Maybe you don't either. I certainly don't anymore. But we are all in a race. The frustrations of seeing others "win" can be intense. But stay the course, keep your head, bow your knees and remain in worship before God. You haven't reached the finish line yet. Determine to worship through the finish line and soon enough things will come clear.

Worship in Action

- Articulating the struggle in your heart may be frightening to you, but God can handle it. Take some moments to settle your heart before the Lord. Collect your thoughts before you speak.
- Now, honestly, what is bugging you about how God seems to be running His world and, in particular, your life? Makes notes; write things down.
- Taking your time and being thorough, lay out your heart before God. Exhaust the perplexity of your heart before Him. Manifest your bewilderment in words addressed to God.
- Having done so, ask God to help you *see*. Ask for insight, wisdom and illumination.
- Know that when you pray such prayers they do not just disappear, but are registered with the Lord. They *stand* before Him and He will answer your request. Determine now to give Him time to do that as He sees fit.
- Explore these matters further by praying through Psalm 73, personalizing and making it your own.

4

Living a Life of Mourning

Psalm 74

There are whole, sweeping sections of the Bible that we sometimes don't want anything to do with. These portions are especially unwelcome when we gather for worship. We simply wouldn't know what to do with them. They are taboo, unthinkable, forbidden. Scholars call these sections *lament*. The dictionary defines lament as "a crying out in grief." To lament is "to mourn aloud" or "to express sorrow . . . often demonstratively."[1]

There's little need to ask why we are uncomfortable with this. We don't have much room for that sort of thing—especially in our corporate worship. We're intent on staying positive, light and happy. People get enough of the negative all week long; we want them to think of church as a joyful, positive, uplifting, inspirational place. Honestly, lament doesn't market well. In market-driven *Church-ianity* it's difficult to see how lament can be anything but a downer.

Interestingly, the Hebrews didn't share this hang-up. By some estimates, as much as one-third of the psalms are designated as lament. Add in the book of Lamentations, major sections of Jeremiah and all of the book of Job, and we can see that God is trying to tell us something—or to help us tell Him something.

Lament doesn't always resolve neatly, and perhaps this factors into some of our discomfort with it. In a world of one-hour television dramas, we are uncomfortable with unresolved pain. The protagonist of the episode may suffer for the first twenty minutes, but after a few commercial breaks, the day is saved and he returns to his normal, relatively happy life.

Psalms 73 and 74 are two well-known prayers of lament. Psalm 73 is a *personal* lament. There, by the end of the prayer, we witness a beautiful resolution. However, Psalm 74 is a *corporate* lament. Here there is no tidy answer to the psalmist's pain, questions, cries and protests. Rather, he seems to drop his quill, abandon the psalm and leave us hanging, wondering and aching for resolution.

Why so much lament in the Scriptures? It's pretty simple really: *Lament is a part of the Bible because suffering is a part of our lives.* In fact lament is an *enormous* part of the Bible because pain is an *enormous* part of our lives in this fallen world.

If we move beyond *attending* worship to *intending* to worship God with the whole of our lives, we'll find that not all worship is the tidy, neat thing we've imagined. True worship is truth-driven—however that may look. All doxology is rooted in theology, but not all worship engages the full breadth of theology. Slice into any life of worship and we'll lay bare a divine-human encounter which is based on truth, but which cannot in that moment fully appreciate, nor take in, the full breadth of truth.

This is one reason we don't generally know how to allow people to process their grief. We want them to do so elsewhere, some place alone, out of the way, unseen, unheard. Grief, one might think, is like some unseemly family dispute, something to be cared for away from the public eye. So we flee lament in our corporate worship and then don't incorporate lament very well into our private worship. Pain is the needle that pierces the dream bubble of life as we'd like to believe it is. We prefer to safely pack away all the jagged edges of life lest they burst our illusions about the life we've inherited. As difficult as it is to realize, living in this present world means experiencing pain. Living a life of worship, therefore, means embracing lament.

How are we to grieve? Enrollment for that course is perennially low. Grief, it seems, is thrust upon us. We will all grieve. Maybe we'll do it well, maybe not. We grieve well when we grieve, mourn and lament *as worship*. How can we do so? Psalm 74 guides our way.

Ask Your Questions

The pattern of the psalm itself invites us to not withhold the questions that inevitably fill our hearts and minds in times of pain. In fact, it models making such queries part of our worship.

Why have You allowed this?

"Why" is unlikely to be a child's first word, but it is liable to be the first question she learns to ask. As a small child, I spent hours upon hours with my dad working on the farm. The nature of the work often gave freedom for one's mind to explore, even while one's hands were busy. Repeatedly I would ask my father "Why ________?" Fill in the blank. It could have been just about anything: "Why do cows chew their cud?" "Why do you wrap the wire around the fencepost that way when you're repairing it?" "Why does the bull run from my Shetland pony?" "Why ________?" Finish the sentence. I did. Repeatedly.

Now that I'm older and have pretty much raised three children, I can appreciate my father's patience. As a boy, I would launch into a barrage of "whys" and he would do his best to answer them for a while. Eventually, he always got to the answer that seemed to put an end to my line of questioning: "It is for little boys to ask questions about." With that, I was lost in another line of thought—*Really! God created that thing or made it work that way just so a little boy could ask his dad about it?* Then, inevitably, again came, "But why?"

The process is somewhat the same in our relationship to our heavenly Father. The torrent of "whys" grows when something goes awry. Loss does not surrender to logic easily. Author and missionary Amy Carmichael once counseled a small child who had just lost her eye in a tragic accident, "Darling, you must never ask God why."[2] Who am I to disagree with such a godly woman? But I feel compelled to wonder if this response isn't ill-advised. Certainly our "why" *may* be misguided, but perhaps it is just that we are too ready to take it up and use it so indiscriminately.

Yet with all these cautions, why (there we go again!) has God placed such prayers in the Psalter? Is it not so we can, in times of deepest distress, find words to unleash our souls toward our heavenly Father? The "whys" of biblical lament exist to aid us in transforming our whys into worship. The psalmist opens his cry:

> 1 O God, why do you cast us off forever?
> Why does your anger smoke against the sheep
> of your pasture?

He goes on to pray:

> 2 Remember your congregation, which you have
> purchased of old,
> which you have redeemed to be the tribe of
> your heritage!
> Remember Mount Zion, where you have dwelt.

> 3 Direct your steps to the perpetual ruins;
> the enemy has destroyed everything in the sanctuary!

By my calculation, the question "why" appears twenty-five times in the book of Job. The story of Job's testing through the loss of his home, children, possessions, wealth and health reminds us that "Why?" is the first and greatest question of the suffering soul.

Someone has said that any person's knowledge can be exhausted by simply asking seven questions in a row—all of them beginning with "Why?"[3] Try it or have someone try it on you. You'll find it works with humans; not so well with God.

When will You put an end to this?

> 10 How long, O God, is the foe to scoff?
> Is the enemy to revile your name forever?

Notice Asaph's concern over time: "forever" (Ps. 73:1, 10, 19) and "how long" (73:9).

If I can't know why, then at least tell me how long!

Traveling when our kids were small was like most any other family's experience. There was the incessant, "How long until we get there?" My wife and I were desperate for an answer that would quell the questions for at least a time. Then one day my wife struck gold. When a little voice arose from the backseat, "How long until we get there?" she replied, "Four Barney shows!" That was all it took; now silence screamed from the backseat. Time calculated in hours and minutes was so abstract as to have no meaning at their young age, but Barney shows—now that's the definition of suffering!

They say that at the speed of light time stands still. Suffering at the speed of life creates a similar phenomenon—it seems to slow down, to drag, to become interminable. Sufferers, ancient and modern, cry with Asaph, "How long, O God?"

Time alone, however, is not the issue. We long to see God's hand move in time and space.

Where is Your power?

> [11] Why do you hold back your hand, your right hand?
> Take it from the fold of your garment and
> destroy them!

As the doctor's little rubber hammer, applied to your knee, produces a reflex kickback, so a blow to the soul creates a reflex that manifests as the questions "Why?" or "When?" or "Where?"

When we sprain an ankle, our body's reflex is to rush fluids to the area, causing swelling. After such an injury, swelling is natural and to some extent unavoidable. It prepares the injured site for healing. But our bodies, in response to the trauma, tend to overdo the reaction and medically we are instructed to control the swelling with ice and pressure.

Questions are the soul's natural response to pain. Your questions are no surprise to God, and they should not be to you. He knows they are your soul's natural response to trauma—an attempt to protect, prevent and heal. We may overdo the questions at times, but they are part of the process of healing, so they must be a part of our worship.

Like me, you've probably noticed our questions often seem to go unanswered. Most questions, at least on the surface, seem to seek answers. However, when it comes to pain, grief, loss and suffering, I have a hunch that our questions are not really seeking answers as much as an Answerer.

Am I alone? Is there someone at the wheel? Does He have a firm plan on where He is taking me?

So, go ahead, ask your questions, but take it a step further.

Articulate Your Pain

We must give expression to that which grieves us. We must open the system. In a closed system no outside resources can be called upon. That which is within stands alone, feeding on itself, brewing, stewing and boiling toward an inevitable eruption. Voicing your pain releases pressure and invites healing breezes of heaven's grace to blow through the stagnant air of circular emotions. This, however, is not a natural response for many. Not all of us were taught to articulate our feelings, and we had few who modeled how to pray with disquieting honesty.

When as a small child I became ill, my mother, like any loving parent, would take me to the doctor. The moment any mention of needing to see the doctor came up, it was as if someone corked me and an emotional pressure began to build. Steadily, it grew, like a foreboding, fearful gas within my soul. *What . . . what if . . . what if . . . I need a–a–a . . . shot?* Perhaps it didn't help that my family always referred to it as a "shot." Why not an injection? "Shot" is what happened to a diseased animal. "Shot" is what you did to a rabbit or a deer. This only added, I assume, to my anxiety.

In any case the dread grew until that fateful moment when the doctor, with his back turned toward me, reached in a drawer and withdrew something. Though his body blocked my view, I knew precisely what he had taken in hand. He carefully prepared the injection, and then came the moment when he turned toward me and I saw it. Down came my pants, over I bent, in went the needle, out came my cry. And boy did I let 'er rip!

This was a great embarrassment to my mother. I know this because in subsequent visits she began to prepare me, to coach me, to goad me, to warn me, to cajole me. All with the end goal of getting me to take the shot without making as much as a peep. Over time, I learned my lesson. The emotion was no less powerful, but I learned to keep my mouth shut, to my mother's great delight.

My mother's pride remained intact until an occasion when my regular doctor was away from the office and I was seen by a new physician. Sure enough, an injection was required. Unaware of the strict protocols established for the procedure, he said to me, "Now, when I poke this into your backside, I want you to scream as loud as you can."

I obliged him. I indulged him. I believe I made him proud.

My mother? Not so much. By the look on her face I thought she might make the doctor cry before we left his office.

Articulating our pain is not our way. In contemporary American culture, we are taught to suffer "like a man." That is to say, shut up, take your medicine and deal with it. Just don't share it with anyone. This is both unhealthy and unbiblical. The laments of the Bible encourage the *articulation* of our pain. Not complaining or whining, mind you, and not to just anyone. The Bible encourages us to give voice to the realities of our hearts *to God.* Prayerful worship is the release valve of the heart.

Psalm 74 models this expression. Notice the Psalmist's pain in the face of *devastation.*

> 3 Direct your steps to the perpetual ruins;
> the enemy has destroyed everything in the sanctuary!

We are not entirely certain what historical events precipitated Psalm 74. But clearly it rose from a national disaster. The evidence seems to suggest it may have occurred when the armies of Nebuchadnezzar, king of Babylon, came to Jerusalem and sacked it in 586 BC.[4] The result was total devastation of the city and Temple. It seemed a total desolation of all that was Israel: God's people, the covenant, the promises, the purpose, vision and glory of God's plan.

It may be difficult for us to understand and identify just what this meant for the Israelites of that day. Picture an ash-laden, bombed-out, burned-out crater where the White House stands. What would such a reality evoke from your heart? That feeling could not compare to the despair of the people of Israel. Their pain went deeper, beyond mere national identity to an ethnic, spiritual and redemptive level as well.

When we look closer, the ruins of verse 3 do not appear to be of recent origin. They are "perpetual ruins." The horror has occurred and the rubble remains as an abiding testament to the devastation. This was not just devastation of their Temple or their city's walls. As a people, they are devastated.

Now, note the psalmist's pain in the face of *defiance.*

> 4 Your foes have roared in the midst of your
> meeting place;
> they set up their own signs for signs.

They didn't just defeat you they demoralized you,—and defied God to stop them!

It was as if their commanding general had walked into the heart of the Holy of Holies and stuck out his chest—a chest upon which the national emblem of Babylon was emblazoned. He raised his arms in victory toward heaven and from the deepest part of his being raised a victory cry like a lion standing over its slain victim, just before devouring it.

By "signs" Asaph most likely refers to military, nationalistic banners. Where worship banners should have been hanging on the walls of the Temple, an enemy's military banners fluttered in the breeze. Militarily and nationally this sight might have been akin to a swastika hanging on the walls of a synagogue today.

Note also the psalmist's expression of pain over destruction.

> 5 They were like those who swing axes
> in a forest of trees.
>
> 6 And all its carved wood
> they broke down with hatchets and hammers.

The Temple was a marvel of the ancient world—ornate, emblazoned in gold, brilliant, glorious, awe inspiring. But into this place of true magnificence came the idol-worshiping hordes of Babylon, treating the holy Temple like an electronics store being looted during a riot. It was a smash and grab affair. The Babylonians grabbed their hatchets, axes, crowbars and claw hammers and started whaling away at the magnificent, hand-carved woodwork of the Temple. It was almost as if they were saying, "Hey, that would look good as crown molding in our family room!" or "A hunk of that on the coffee table back home will make a nice conversation piece!"

Listen to the psalmist cry out over *defilement*.

> 7 They set your sanctuary on fire;
> they profaned the dwelling place of your name,
> bringing it down to the ground.

The Babylonians were not content merely with devastating the Jewish people, with defying God, nor with destroying the Temple. They realized that to the Jews the Temple was more than the object of their national pride. It was a holy place. Destruction was not sufficient, they had to defile it as well. They did this, not just by stripping the Temple down to the stone, but also by setting it ablaze.

Earlier this week, a dear pastor-friend sent word that his church building was burned to the ground by an arsonist. It is a feeling for which it is difficult to find words. His e-mail, significantly, bore the subject line "I *tell* you what" (emphasis added).

Do you see how important that word is? There must be an expression of the . . . oh, what is the word?

Emotion?

I'm not sure *emotion* is strong enough. Emotion is what you experience when you smash your thumb or your football team wins or when you've just enjoyed a delicious meal. But this is deeper. It goes beyond mere feelings.

Having stood with his church family amid the smoldering ruins of their building and the rich history of God's gracious dealings with them that it symbolized, my friend wrote, "Many people have asked how we are doing and all of that. I would be lying if I said all was well. It is hard because so many people comment about it being 'just a building'—I get that and I agree, but we do mourn the loss. It means something to us, we cannot ignore that."

Precisely.

I have to wonder if that is something of how it was for the ancient Israelites as they contemplated their devastated city and Temple.

Even if all is not consumed, it is ruined. The smell is horrid and irremovable. Indeed, the holy place of Israel was brought "down to the ground." It was run through the mud, ground into the dirt, reduced to rubble. And it was done in a taunting spirit of "so where's your God now?"

Listen also as the psalmist gives expression to the experience of *domination.*

> 8 They said to themselves, "We will utterly subdue them";
> they burned all the meeting places of God in the land.

The devastation, destruction and defilement had to be total! They utterly subdued them. They took their place, their practice and their pride. For them, entire subjugation was the only acceptable outcome.

And in the face of all this, when the sound of axes hacking away at the woodwork dies out, after the triumph cry of defiance is past, when the sound of flames crackling in the sanctuary of God have flickered out, what then do we hear from heaven?

Silence.

> 9 We do not see our signs;
> there is no longer any prophet,
> and there is none among us who knows how long.

The expression "our signs" is a translation of the same Hebrew word used in verse 4. There it designated the Babylonian nationalistic, military banners or "signs." Here, in verse 9, it most likely signals not physical banners, but the kinds of "signs" a divinely-chosen people might expect to see as evidence that is true—signs like a prophet speaking a timely word from God or miraculous signs that testify to His concern for His people.

But, sadly, there is "no longer any prophet." There is no word from God. Previously, God told them this was coming: " 'Behold, the days are coming,' declares the Lord God, 'when I will send a famine on the land—not a famine of bread, nor a thirst for water, but of hearing the words of the

LORD'" (Amos 8:11). "Disaster comes upon disaster; rumor follows rumor. They seek a vision from the prophet, while the law perishes from the priest and counsel from the elders" (Ezek. 7:26). But as for the present, there is no word from God. And "there is none among us who knows how long" (Ps. 74:9). Will it be "forever" (74:1, 10, 19)?

Why bother with all this historical detail? After all, most of us aren't Jews. We don't live in the sixth century BC, we've never been to Jerusalem and we certainly never saw Solomon's Temple.

No, but maybe you have been the victim of childhood abuse, sexual assault or criminal violence. Or perhaps someone you love has been subject to such atrocities. Maybe you've truly been trashed by someone you trusted. Or you've faced the humiliation of financial collapse. Possibly you've been laden with the diagnosis of mental illness or in some other way your soul has been violated, abused and traumatized.

We may not be Jews in the sixth century before Christ, but we all eventually need to articulate the pain that comes from our experiences.

However, in seeking to articulate our pain, we seem to go to one of two extremes. We may misapply and overuse the strong language of lament by flippantly calling upon extreme words like "devastation" when they do not really apply. The result is that we have no words left at our disposal when true devastation strikes. The people around us then treat the genuine devastation just as we've trained them to respond to our pseudo-devastation all along. Like the boy who cried "wolf!" when there was no wolf, our overused and misapplied words may leave us unable to articulate in meaningful ways the actual pain of authentic devastation. This, of course, only compounds the real devastation we now face.

On the other hand, perhaps we go awry because we fail to articulate the reality of our pain. We've been trained to just "deal with it," to "shut up and do your job!" We've never acquired and developed an emotional vocabulary. Thus, we utilize the same few words to describe what we feel in a variety of experiences. The result is imprecise lament and thus a vague connection with God and an inhibited emotional release.

Let's stop for a moment and take stock. If we are to live a life of worship we must, at times, embrace a life of lament. To do this, we must ask our questions and articulate our pain. The point is that we must do this in such a way that it *becomes an act of worship*! Lament is not the goal of worship. It is not the final act in the drama of worship. But lament is *part* of worship, a part that cannot be left out without robbing worship of all it is meant to be.

Believe it or not, there are other, more positive parts of lament. One essential part begins with acknowledgement.

Acknowledge God's Past

The questions are fresh. The pain is real. But the psalmist's focus changes. He raises his eyes from self and personal pain and gazes, by faith, upon God. The text signals this by nine times addressing "you," referring to God (Ps. 74:13–17). The focus is no longer upon the psalmist (see 74:1–11) or the one who takes up his prayer as his own. It is now shifted away from earth and its pains to heaven and the One who sits upon His throne, ruling over all that transpires below.

Despite the devastation, destruction, defilement and domination, the worshiper's memory has not been disabled. Looking back, he must confess that God has proven powerful and faithful in the past. He may not be able to explain why that faithfulness doesn't appear to be present now or why that unlimited power is not unleashed at the moment, yet he does admit that *God has acted for His people*. He looks back over the history of God's dealings with Israel—particularly the deliverance out of Egypt and provisions in the wilderness on the way to the Promised Land.

> 12 Yet God my King is from of old,
> working salvation in the midst of the earth.
>
> 13 You divided the sea by your might;[5]
> you broke the heads of the sea monsters on
> the waters.
>
> 14 You crushed the heads of Leviathan;[6]
> you gave him as food for the creatures of the
> wilderness.
>
> 15 You split open springs and brooks;[7]
> you dried up ever-flowing streams.[8]

Similarly, he recalls that *God has acted in His creation*.

> 16 Yours is the day, yours also the night;
> you have established the heavenly lights and
> the sun.
>
> 17 You have fixed all the boundaries of the earth;
> you have made summer and winter.

It is almost as if the psalmist prays,

O God, despite everything that has befallen me, the sun came up this morning—and You did that! The stars still shine this night, even if clouds have obscured my view of them. And it was You who told them where to dance and parade their light. You established the national boundaries of every people on the earth. Ultimately, it is not their armed forces who maintain those borders, it is You, O God! Despite my personal devastation, the seasons keep right on moving, changing on schedule, and You are the One who leads them out and tucks them in bed when their time is done.

How might this look for us?

Certainly we can also look upon God as the Creator of and Sovereign over creation. The New Testament tells us to remember that Jesus was the agent of creation and that He sustains it all even now. We also do well to remember God's provision in leading us out of the bondage of sin and into eternal life in Jesus. Take some time to recount afresh the wonders of your Savior and of the salvation He has brought to you. These things are true, whatever else happens. Turn again to Romans 8:31–39—read, memorize and pray it again and again. Never let go of the prayer of Psalm 119:68: "You are good, and what you do is good" (NIV). Doggedly confess, as did my friend John Stumbo in the midst of a physically devastating and life-threatening disease, "God is in this and God is good!"[9]

Ask for God's Intervention

In all of this, don't be timid in asking God to *act*. Request that He respond, do, manifest and move His hand. The psalmist did when he cried out: *Remember this tragedy!* Note Asaph's repeated cries: "Remember your congregation," "Remember Mount Zion," "Remember this, O LORD" and "O God, . . . remember how the foolish scoff at you" (Ps. 74:2, 18, 22). See also his pleas: "Do not forget the life of your poor forever" and "Do not forget the clamor of your foes" (Ps. 74:19, 23).

Shortly after the tragedy of 9/11, many in America vowed "We will not forget!" The cry was emblazoned on many an automobile bumper, but we don't see so many of those anymore. We have forgotten. Other pressures are felt more acutely.

Other sociological forces demand our attention. The sense of violation and the attending outrage we felt have been tempered by a climate of political correctness and tinted to a new hue by other more immediate concerns.

It is not only our tragedies we forget, but also, conveniently, our failures. How well I remember that late January day when I stood in the Kurapaty forest outside Minsk, the capital of Belarus. The winter wind whispered a sad ode as it slipped between the branches of majestic pines laden with snow. Low swags in the earth—evident even beneath the snow-pack—bore testimony to a gruesome and grizzly past, the only grave markers remaining for people too numerous to count. This quiet place had been the scene of countless deaths during the Communist purges. Over a period of years, an average of twelve truckloads of people a day were brought to this spot, a gun put to their head and their earthly existence ended—intellectuals, college professors, professionals, clergy, anyone who might be ratted out as an "enemy of the people." The economic ruin and vast starvation made the going price for turning in an "enemy of the people" too attractive for many Belarusians to pass up. Neighbors, family members and many innocents were sold for a mess of stew.[10]

As I stood there, blanketed in the winter silence, I wondered why I'd never heard this story before. The answer is simple—because there are those who want the truth to disappear, for the horrors to be blotted from all memory banks.

Remember our suffering!

> 2 Remember your congregation, which you have
> purchased of old,
> which you have redeemed to be the tribe of
> your heritage!
> *Remember Mount Zion, where you have dwelt!*

3 Direct your steps to the perpetual ruins;
the enemy has destroyed everything in the sanctuary!

Remember our persecutors!

18 Remember this, O LORD, how the enemy scoffs,
and a foolish people reviles your name.

23 Do not forget the clamor of your foes,
the uproar of those who rise against you,
which goes up continually!

Similarly, the psalmist cries: *Rescue Your people!*

19 Do not deliver the soul of your dove to the wild beasts;
do not forget the life of your poor forever.

11 Why do you hold back your hand, your right hand?
Take it from the fold of your garment and destroy them!

Do You hear these prayers? God, get Your hands out of Your pockets and do something!

Ask God to act on your behalf or on behalf of those in need. Certainly, bow to His will and timing. But remember, He wants you to ask for His hand to move on behalf of His people.

And the psalmist calls, *Regard Your covenant!*

20 Have regard for the covenant,
for the dark places of the land are full of the habitations of violence.

21 Let not the downtrodden turn back in shame;
let the poor and needy praise your name.

He refers to God's covenant with Abraham, the promise to make of him a great nation, a nation through whom the

Messiah would come and demonstrate God's glory and extend God's grace to all of creation. As the God of covenant, He is uniquely the God of covenant faithfulness—of loyal, promise-defined mercy and love. God's covenant with Abraham is now being fulfilled in the new covenant promised by God (see Jeremiah 31) and realized through Jesus Christ. As children of God, through faith in Jesus Christ, we have the responsibility and privilege to call upon God to keep His covenant with us as His children.

A few weeks ago I led a prayer gathering. As we began, I asked each person to introduce him or herself. But I asked them not to say, "Hi, I'm John." Rather, I requested that they identify themselves by what is true of them "in Christ." So, as we went around the circle, person after person introduced himself by saying something like . . . "Hi, I'm dead to sin in Christ," "Hi, I'm risen to new life with Christ," "Hi, sin is no longer my master," "Hi, I'm the one Jesus calls friend" or "Hi, I'm indwelt by the Holy Spirit."

Identity is defined by covenant. Not circumstances. Not breeding. Not experiences. Not body shape or hairline. But identity framed by covenant realities. That would change some things, wouldn't it? Pain is an invitation to stand by faith on the ground given by covenant with God Himself through the blood of His Son.

It may seem counterintuitive, but when catastrophe, pain, suffering, hardship, trial and misery show up, it is God's call to worship. Pain is God's invitation to ask our questions, articulate our pain, acknowledge God's past and ask for God's intervention.

It might not be today, but the time will come when living a life of worship will require of us the worship that can only be expressed through lament. We only take up lament when we've encountered bad news. But here's the good news about lament: *Suffering and pain don't have to signal the end of a life of worship*. In fact, the prominent place the Bible gives to lament is proof that our deepest encounters with God may come wrapped in the deepest pains of life.

Worship in Action

- Lament, by definition, needs to be expressed, articulated, spoken. Arrange to be alone in a place where you'll be free to vocalize your heart to God.
- What is your hurt? Your complaint before God? Ask Him to help you identify and pinpoint your wound precisely.
- God's ways are beyond understanding. They are often shrouded in mystery. There are questions that remain. What are yours? Write them down. Be specific. Then express them—allowing your emotions to bring authenticity to your prayers.
- Give expression to the pain that seems to stand between you and God. Speaking it out before God brings it into the light. There, in the light, its power is dissipated. Is it devastation? Then describe it to God in prayer. Do you feel defiance toward him? Tell Him. He can handle it; and you need to be free of it. Exhaust yourself before God in this. Don't rush this step. Do this thoroughly.
- Now give yourself the space of quietness, just lingering in God's presence. When you are through this stage, ask God to bring to your mind the many ways He has proven His faithfulness in your life. Jot them down as they come to mind. Give yourself time. Verbally recount God's goodness to you. Begin now to speak out words of thanksgiving.

- Finally, humbly ask God to intervene in your current crisis. Ask Him what you wish. Bow to His wisdom and will. Tell God you want Him more than you want His actions; but ask Him to act, to intervene, to move and to make Himself known in the circumstances that concern you.

5

Living a Life of Patience

Psalm 75

If the thoughts of your heart were twisted into the shape of a question mark and presented to God, what would your prayer sound like? A fair share of them would echo Asaph's prayer in the previous psalm: "How long, O God . . . ?" (74:10). How long, O God, until You . . . answer my prayer? Heal my friend? Stop the bullies? Provide a marriage partner? Change my spouse? Give me a job? Lift this depression? Change my circumstances? Get me out of here?

While Psalm 74:10 raises the question, Psalm 75 provides an answer.[1]

In form, Psalm 75 is the outline of a worship service.[2] It begins with what we, corporately, say to God as we come before Him in worship (see 75:1). What follows constitutes what God says to us in worship (see 75:2–8). This includes Scripture, God's revelation to man (see 75:2–5), and a sermon, man's exposition of what God has revealed in Scripture (see 75:6–8). Then the psalm closes with what I individually say in response to God's revelation of Himself. Worship is made up of the intricate, rhythmic weaving of revelation and response. God speaks. We respond.

But what of those times when God does not seem to act? When it appears there will be no move from heaven? No word from God? Too often for our liking the question is: *How am I to worship God while waiting on him?* The question is not: Will it be necessary to wait? Wait we will. Waiting is part of God's core curriculum; it is not elective. The real question is: *In my waiting, will I worship?*

Psalm 75 helps us answer that question. It does so by telling us what God is saying to us in times of waiting and by giving us words with which we may respond to Him in worship.

What God Says While We Wait in Worship

God reveals five truths to us while we wait upon Him in worship. Listen to what He proclaims:

- *My justice is timely.*
- *My providence is constant.*
- *My warning is consistent.*
- *My rights are exclusive.*
- *My judgment is thorough.*

For many, the question remains, "How long, O God . . . ?" (Ps. 74:10). God responds directly to the question: *My justice is timely.*

> 2 At the set time that I appoint,
> I will judge with equity.

God will move "at the set time." The Hebrew expression elsewhere refers to the changing of seasons (see Gen. 1:14), the annual "appointed" feasts of Israel (see Lev. 23:2), even to events of the end times—"time, times, and half a time" (Dan. 12:7).[2] Just as the seasons change right on time, just as the holidays roll around without fail, so God will bring all things to their appointed end at the appointed time.

As regards His justice, God says, "I will judge with equity." In this case, the "I" is emphatic. *At a time I have determined as correct, I will step out of the shadows and into the spotlight.*

In one sense, sin is its own judgment. "The wrath of God *is being revealed* from heaven against all the godlessness and wickedness of people" (Rom. 1:18, NIV). In some way which is not entirely explained to us, God is currently pouring out His wrath upon sin. There is a reciprocating suffering that sin brings upon those who practice it.[3] Some sin is judged in this lifetime. All sin will be judged.

Yes, but *when*?

This is the great question; one for which we all want an answer. It is what the disciples of Jesus wished to know. "As he sat on the Mount of Olives, the disciples came to him privately, saying, 'Tell us, when will these things be, and what will be the sign of your coming and of the end of the age?'" (Matt. 24:3). As Jesus answered their question, He warned us all, "But concerning that day and hour no one knows, not even the angels of heaven, nor the Son, but the Father only" (24:36).

In a most fundamental way, God has already judged our sins. He did this in Jesus upon the cross. "At just the right time, when we were still powerless, Christ died for the ungodly" (Rom. 5:6, NIV). Christ endured the full punishment of God's wrath against our sin that we might never have to (see Rom. 3:23–26). So that now, "If we confess our sins, he is faithful and just to forgive us our sins and to cleanse us from all unrighteousness" (1 John 1:9).

In our waiting God also says to us: *My providence is constant.*

> 3 When the earth totters, and all its inhabitants,
> it is I who keep steady its pillars.

The psalmist looks about and observes the wicked winning. The world as he has known it "totters." Another worshiper once wondered aloud: "Behold, the wicked . . . ; if the foundations are destroyed, what can the righteous do?" (Ps. 11:2-3). It appears that the very foundations of moral order, the building blocks of society, are crumbling, and ungodliness has permeated the culture.

Today, the basics are being questioned. What is marriage? What constitutes a family? What is an acceptable sexual orientation?

And we wonder, *is nothing sacred?*

Unfortunately, no. Not anymore. Not here. Not now.

The entire culture seems to have reached the tipping point. We find ourselves tottering—the moral ground beneath our feet roiling and rocking, and everything built upon it is coming down around us.

At such times, God says, *It is I who keep steady its pillars.* It is a picture of all reality—all society, all the earth, all nations, indeed, everything—built and resting upon "pillars." God reaches out from some fixed point beyond perceivable reality and with a firm hand steadies and keeps it all from falling in upon itself.

God also says to us in our waiting: *My warning is consistent.*

> 4 I say to the boastful, "Do not boast,"
> and to the wicked, "Do not lift up your horn;
>
> 5 do not lift up your horn on high,
> or speak with haughty neck."

The arrogant one's "horn" is a symbol of military strength or personal power. It probably calls upon the familiar image of an ox's horn, just as the "neck" pictures the power of the ox to wield that horn with destructive power.

Asaph's image strikes a chord with something sounding from my memory bank. When I was a small child, our family owned a bull that had been honored with the formidable name Loadstar. The very mention of it sent shivers up my spine and made my knees turn to jelly. Few fears were more consistent than that of being caught alone in the barn lot with Loadstar. My father fueled my anxieties by telling fearsome stories of bull attacks from the past.

I don't spend much time around bulls anymore—at least not that kind. I have, however, discovered that there are those in life who believe that their power and pride demand something more than they deserve. God reminds us that the arrogant and proud, those who believe they can live life as they wish and will not have to answer for it, are taking a gamble they cannot win.

I lived in near daily terror of Loadstar. But, had I the perspective to see it, God was giving me a regular reminder that such power is not all it may appear to be. At the time, I owned a diminutive Shetland pony, whom I had named Sandy. It was not uncommon to see Sandy, when he had the chance, chasing after Loadstar and putting him to flight. My tiny pony had buffaloed the massive bull.

Similarly, the Scriptures remind us that not all is as it appears. God, in our waiting, also reminds us: *My rights are exclusive.*

> 6 For not from the east or from the west
> and not from the wilderness comes lifting up,
>
> 7 but it is God who executes judgment,
> putting down one and lifting up another.

God alone is Judge. Only God can "lift up." And God most certainly will "put down" all who defy Him. By "lifting up" (Ps. 75:4, 5, 6, 7, 10), God refers to granting honor and success; by "putting down" (75:7), judgment, disaster and loss. The conferring of either is a right and prerogative that God shares with no one.

Judgment, in our current culture, is the worst of all possible sins. To judge another is deemed almost worse than murder, robbery, kidnapping or abuse. Culture claims, "No one has the right to judge!" Which is, of course, a judgment. But never mind that!

Though most wouldn't verbalize it, there are those who think this extends even to God. To speak of God's right to judge, His promise to judge, and—heaven forbid!—actual acts of judgment is, to most, just a bit embarrassing. Intimidated by the culture, many treat God's judgment as an unfortunate family trait to be kept from the public's eye and from open conversation.

This is, frankly, a bit ironic. We are at the moment overrun with TV talent shows. Every network seems to have some version of a singing or dancing competition. Every show sports a panel of—*gulp!*—judges. Many invite the live audience and those watching at home to text in their judgment! We gobble it up, never sensing the irony of it all.

But irony and embarrassment aside, look where you wish for help in succeeding with life and avoiding disaster and judgment. You can look to the "east," you can reach out to the "west," you can wildly swing your hand out to the south ("wilderness"). But there is no one who can help you when God determines you need to be brought down.

Finally, God says to us in our waiting: *My judgment is thorough.*

8 For in the hand of the Lord there is a cup
with foaming wine, well mixed,
and he pours out from it,
and all the wicked of the earth
shall drain it down to the dregs.

Throughout Scripture, the "cup" is an image of judgment. To "drink" the "cup" is to experience God's judgment. The cup is "foaming" because it has stupefying spices stirred into it. Often we hear this imagery from the prophets. It is prominent also in Revelation: "God remembered Babylon the great, to make her drain the cup of the wine of the fury of his wrath" (Rev. 16:19).

The point is that God's judgment is certain and it will be thorough. This includes and culminates in the ultimate judgment of hell. *Oh my! Another embarrassing Scriptural antique!*

Today, even if one affirms in theory the reality of hell, no one can quite imagine God actually sending anyone there.

But if the Scriptures are true, hell is real. Hell is a place—not simply a state of mind. Hell is eternal—not merely temporary; nor is it annihilation. Hell is unspeakably horrible—the imagery of the Bible is true and real. Yes, there is poetic description, but the poetic arises from and points to a definite reality. The device of poetry is designed to take our minds to the farthest reaches of the worst misery humanly conceivable, and then invites us to peer beyond even that into the unbounded horror of an infinite God's holy wrath.

But remember, there is another place this imagery of judgment is used. It was in the garden of Gethsemane. There, wrestling in agony with the full knowledge of what the Father's will required of Him, Jesus prayed, "My Father, if it be possible, let this cup pass from me; nevertheless, not as I will, but as you will" (Matt. 26:39).

Jesus left the disciples behind, walked to the edge of hell and looked at what it would take to keep you from going there. That night in prayer, Jesus evaluated the price of freeing you from your sins and rescuing you from their judgment. Quaking at the reality of what He saw, Jesus cried, "Father, if there is any way . . ."

But there was no other way. Sin is real. God is holy and just.

So Jesus, God the Son in human flesh, went to the cross and allowed the Father to judge our sins in Him, that such judgment might never be visited upon us.

When waiting upon God, when impatience rises, when our perspective begins to fail, recall these five truths: His justice is timely, His providence is constant, His warning is consistent, His rights are exclusive and His judgment thorough.

David was right to counsel himself, "For God alone, O my soul, wait in silence, for my hope is from him" (Ps. 62:5). The sage reminds us, "Be not rash with your mouth, nor let your heart be hasty to utter a word before God, for God is in heaven and you are on earth. Therefore let your words be few" (Eccles. 5:2). But Hosea was also correct. There is a time to "take with you words and return to the LORD" (Hos. 14:2).

We must listen well in worship. But worship is not divine initiative alone. It includes also our human response to that divine revelation. When the time comes, what should be our words in worship?

What We Say While We Wait in Worship

By faith we confess to God: *We rejoice that You are near.*

> 1 We give thanks to you, O God;
> we give thanks, for your name is near.

God's "name" is another way of referring to God Himself—to His person, His nature, His character. There are times when God *feels* distant. It is not a distance of space, but of dimension. Our perception is that God is not close at hand because we don't feel like He is near. Worship recalibrates our perceptions and conforms them to reality. Indeed, "he is actually not far from each one of us" (Acts 17:27).

As physical beings in a physical world, we are used to measuring things by physical distance. In the spiritual world, reality is measured by spiritual distance. Calculating spiritual truth by physical distance distorts that truth. It is akin to asking for a pound of love or a cup of joy. Both joy and love are real, but they are not subject to physical measurements.

Jesus' work before the cross was to make the name of God known. He said, "I have manifested your name to the people whom you gave me out of the world" (John 17:6). This is still His work. Again Jesus said, "I made known to them your name, and I will continue to make it known" (John 17:26). In the Person of Jesus, God has come near. God hung flesh on His name and in that earthly body the eternal God has revealed His person and nature.

Having died, risen and ascended, Jesus sent the Holy Spirit to continue to make His name, person, presence and nature even more intimately known to us. So, while waiting on God, we gather in worship and give thanks that God is near to us, nearer than He was even to Asaph and his descendants.

That nearness is not dependent upon location (a tabernacle, temple or church building), but upon relationship—relationship with God through Jesus made real through the abiding presence and ministry of the Holy Spirit. Thus, worship is not primarily about going *to* worship, but being *in* worship.

We should speak this with confidence and gratitude as we worship God.

Similarly, in worship we tell God: *We confess that we have seen Your hand.* Asaph asserted, "We recount your wondrous deeds" (Ps. 75:1).

While we are waiting on God to act—to perform new "wondrous deeds" that we desperately need to see from His hand—we busy ourselves remembering and recounting what He has already done.

For the worshiping Jew, that meant recounting God's glorious interventions, acts and doings in the lives of people and events like the following:

- Creation
- Noah and the flood
- Abraham, Isaac, Jacob and Joseph
- Moses and the deliverance from Egypt
- The wilderness provisions
- Joshua and possessing the Promised Land
- The Judges, Samuel, Saul, David and Solomon
- The kings of Israel and Judah
- The exile and restoration to the land

As Christians, that means mentally recalling and verbally celebrating these great acts of God:

- All of the above, plus the following
- Breaking the prophetic silence by sending and speaking through John the Baptist
- The incarnation

- Jesus' miracle-studded life
- Jesus' death on the cross, resurrection and ascension
- Pentecost—the sending of the Holy Spirit and the creation of the church
- The mandate to take the gospel to the world and to make disciples of all peoples
- Every other individual act of God in advancing this gospel down through the annals of church history
- The many individual ways—large and seemingly small—in which God has extended His grace, power, wisdom, strength and love into our personal lives and those of our families

Remembrance is an enduring principle of worship throughout all God's dealings with His people—*while you wait for what you need from God, remember and recount what God has already done.*

When God moved our family from Wisconsin to Ohio, our children were twelve, ten and three years of age. They were asked to leave behind the only life they'd ever known. In a cardboard box stashed in our front closet, sitting amid hundreds of other photographs, there is one that evokes great emotion in me. It is a picture of my wife, Julie, and our then ten-year-old son, Joe. It was taken our first night in our new home—a home still devoid of furniture and any of the physical things that had made up their lives from birth. In the picture, Julie and Joe are sitting together in an empty house—on the floor of the empty kitchen. Together they are looking through a memory book of pictures prepared and given to us by dear friends in Wisconsin before our departure.

When I see that picture, I see the stark contrast between the previous fourteen years, chock-full of incredible acts of God on our behalf, and the current reality of an empty house in a strange town, surrounded only by one another and the presence of God. Our memory banks were full, but our future was blank. When I think of all the emotion wrapped up in that move—all the wonderful memories of God's grace in us and work through us in those previous years, all the uncertainty and fear of what lay ahead of us—and then see my young son and dear wife pouring over memories from the past, it is a profoundly moving experience. Now, with the perspective of over a dozen years in that new home and ministry, I see that same picture and want to emblazon this caption beneath it: God *has*. God *will*.

Isn't this the tension of worship and faith? God *has*. God *will*. God has been gracious; He will be gracious. God has defended us; He will defend us yet again. God has been present; He is present still. God has demonstrated His faithfulness to His promises; not one good word of His promises will fail us now, or ever. *God has. God will.* This is our confession in worship.

Furthermore, we confess in worship: *I affirm Your word in faith.*

"But I will declare it forever" (Ps. 75:9).

Declare what? What is the "it" that we must declare?

What, in the context of the psalm, comes immediately before? God's Word! He has spoken directly, through His Word (see Ps. 75:2–5), and indirectly, through careful exposition of that Word (see 75:6–8).

He has done so not just in a *general* way. We do not merely hold high the Bible and say, "I believe God's Word!" But God has spoken to us *specifically*. We hold high that Bible and confess we believe God's Word, but then we open it, read its content, dive into its actual words. We see what they mean for us in our present circumstances. And, having done so, we confess, "I believe God when He says . . ."

Here in Psalm 75 that word has been about God's judgment on the ungodly. Do you affirm God's Word on this?

But God's Word speaks to every situation we face. And it does so *personally*. My affirmation of what Scripture says must be just as personal and specific. The "I" is emphatic: "*I* will declare it." A number of translations render it, "But as for me, I will . . ." (NLT, NASB, NIV).

It is your intent to live by this credo: "I say what God says." The question before us all is: Will I say what God says about success and failure? Do I say what God says about heaven and hell? Do I say what God says about salvation? About hope? About sex, marriage and family? About work and leisure? And about every other thing to which God has spoken in His Word?

In worship we also say to God: *I worship Your perfections.*

"I will sing praises to the God of Jacob" (see 75:9).

I realize it may sound odd to speak of God's perfections. It's not how most today would speak of such things. But to speak of God's perfections is simply another way of speaking of His attributes—of who He is and what He has revealed of Himself.

The psalmist says he will do this "to the God of Jacob." What does that mean? Many things, actually. But at least this much:

- God is the God of *purpose*—God patiently dealt with Jacob until Jacob realized that he was not the point, God was . . . and is.

- God is the God of *covenant*—it was not about what Jacob brought to the table, but what God provided.
- God is the God of *promises*—it was not about how faithful Jacob would be, but how faithful God would be.
- God is the God of *mercy*—Jacob was a rascal, and we all have a little of Jacob in us.
- God is the God of *hope*—God wouldn't leave Jacob as Jacob, but patiently and persistently transformed him until he became Israel.

So we worship as we wait by keeping our eyes on God—by speaking of God and who He is, as well as what His purposes are and why He has shown us such mercy.

Then also, painful though it may be, we say to God in worship: *I rest in Your judgment.*

> 10 All the horns of the wicked I will cut off,
> but the horns of the righteous shall be lifted up.

There is some debate about who is doing the speaking here. Is it God? Possibly. Or is it the psalmist (or the individual worshiper taking up his psalm)? This seems more likely, in my estimation.

Just what, then, is the psalmist confessing about God's judgment? Interpreters focus on three possibilities. Is it that the psalmist/worshiper joins God in judging those God condemns?[5] Is he testifying to what God will yet do—"God will do as He says"?[6] Or is it a picture of the psalmist affirming God's own word of judgment?

> 4 I say to the boastful, "Do not boast,"
> and to the wicked, "Do not lift up your horn;

> 5 do not lift up your horn on high,
> or speak with haughty neck."[7]

Perhaps it is all three. For in worship I affirm the fact that God will do as He promised. God opposes all evil. God, in Jesus, took the judgment of our sin upon Himself. I personally rest myself in His judgment of my sin in Jesus. I will announce this good news, even as I warn of impending judgment upon the unrepentant.

God is the Judge. I will rest in my role as worshiper and wait upon Him. "Vengeance is mine, I will repay, says the Lord" (Rom. 12:19). Worship is mine; vengeance is His. This I confess and in this I will rest as a waiting worshiper.

Still the question persists: "How long, O God, until You ________?" It simply won't go away. Not in this life. But know this: if you are holding back your worship until a more satisfying answer comes, you will never become a worshiper of God at all.

Here's the thing—waiting is not an impediment to worship. Rather, *worship is the answer to waiting*. Worship is to waiting what *oxygen* is to life, what *exercise* is to health, what *yellow* is to the rainbow. Without yellow, a rainbow isn't a rainbow. Without exercise, you won't have health. The absence of oxygen soon spells the absence of life.

Waiting without worshiping is like trying to see without eyes, hear without ears or stand without a skeletal system. It just doesn't work. For waiting is at the very heart of worship.

Wait you will. The question is for whom and for what. Answer that and you'll find the one you truly worship.

Worship in Action

- Impatience is the problem, so patience in prayer will be part of the answer. Thus, make sure to block out some time and space where you will not be interrupted as you seek God.
- After an unhurried time of settling yourself in God's presence, outline to Him the matters which make you anxious and which seem to demand immediate action from Him. Be thorough. Be convincing. Be honest.
- Having done so, be still. Tell God you will simply worship Him now with your stillness. No demanding. No fidgeting. No suggesting, cajoling or whining. Content yourself to be in the presence of Him who rules time and all that transpires in it.
- As you linger consciously in God's presence, reflect again upon what God is saying to you in verses 2–8.
- Turn God's words back to Him in worship—humbly and by faith affirm that His justice is timely, His providence is constant, His warnings are consistent, His rights are exclusive and His judgment is thorough. Admit to Him when you are doing this *by faith* and are unable to do this *by sight*. But affirm Him in these facts.

- Now simply rejoice in God's nearness to you. He is not distant. He must not be roused awake from across some vast space that separates Him from you. He is immediate. He is attentive. He knows. He cares. He is caring and tending to you even this very moment. Thank Him.
- Recount to God the ways you have seen His hand move on your behalf in the past. Remember—verbally—His past faithfulnesses to you, to His Word, to His covenant with you.
- Affirm God's Word by faith. Take up specific—and circumstantially appropriate—promises from the Bible. Read them out before God and tell Him you believe He is going to keep these promises in your life.
- Recount God's attributes. Reflect upon them out loud before Him. Praise Him for being this kind of God.
- And now tell God that you rest yourself in however He chooses to resolve the issues that are in play here. Release them into His hands and tell Him that however He chooses to resolve or not resolve these issues, and in whatever time He chooses to do so, you trust His judgment.
- Ask that God fill you afresh with His own living presence through the Holy Spirit. Breathe in His presence, life and love. Be at rest.

6

Living a Life of Submission

Psalm 76

Okay, so a while back I was reading the recommended procedures in case of airplane pilot incapacitation.

Don't ask. Remember, you're only three clicks away from information you never dreamed of reading—or needing.

Trouble is, now I'm a little worried. Then, just a couple of days ago, it happened. *It actually happened!*

Think of it. You're approximately halfway to your destination, cruising at thirty thousand feet, enjoying your complimentary soft drink and pretzels, when a crew member's voice comes over the loudspeaker asking if there happens to be a physician aboard.

All 161 fellow-passengers appear to be in fine health. *Um, who is in need of a physician?*

Sadly, it was the captain of the plane. He didn't make it, despite the stellar assistance of two doctors who happened to be aboard.[1] Fortunately, the copilot was able to safely land the plane.

But doesn't that make you wonder?

The basics in case the pilot goes down while the plane is still up are, I suppose, fairly obvious:

- Remove the incapacitated pilot.
- Take control of the plane.
- *After* successfully landing the plane, turn to help the pilot.

Any real help for the pilot follows a whole lot of contingencies.

These instructions are designed for the cockpit personnel, of course. A location I'm not likely to find myself.

So, my question is this: What if you have no access to the controls and those who—you know—control them? What about the folks in the main cabin of the aircraft? Should the aircraft suddenly become bereft of its pilot, we surely would be able to feel the plane's odd movements. We long ago learned that you never approach the cabin door.

Have you ever wondered if everyone behind that door is all right? Have they succumbed to some disaster? Is anyone even at the controls? Is there a hand on the stick, steering the plane?

And it's not just airplanes, is it?

It's all of life. It can leave you asking these kinds of questions as well. The cockpit of the universe is shrouded in even thicker, more mysterious darkness. Sometimes the movements of life make you wonder if anyone has their hand on the stick guiding history itself.

Now, drop the emergency airplane manual and thumb through your Bible to find Psalm 76. You'll discover it enables us to steer a course of worship in such times.

While we're still in the airplane mode, picture the landscape of the psalm from high above. You'll notice this song divides perfectly in half—two halves of six verses each (verses 1–6 and 7–12). Now divide each in half again—four quarters, each of three verses (verses 1–3, 4–6, 7–9, 10–12).

The first half of the psalm deals with the particulars; the second half deals with principles. We learn first that something specific has happened—something that would (at least momentarily) make one wonder who is at the controls of the universe. But then, in the second half of the psalm, things turn out great. God shows up!

That is all very wonderful. But before we jubilate too much, may I ask: What about those moments just before God does show up? That moment right before God moves His mighty hand on your behalf, but when you're still wondering if He ever will. What does worship look like when nothing but God will do, but there is no sign He's on His way?

No doubt about it, the particulars of life can make worship a challenge!

But don't forget those principles in the second half of the psalm. These principles help us draw lines of clear application from the particulars of what God once did to the specifics of what we may face in other situations and at other times.

Asaph reminds us that when the world appears out of control a good memory is a worshiper's best friend. So, remember…

God Has Revealed Himself

> 1 In Judah God is known;
> his name is great in Israel.
>
> 2 His abode has been established in Salem,
> his dwelling place in Zion.

God has made Himself known *in a particular place*. He is known "In Judah . . . in Israel . . . in Salem . . . in Zion." It is there that God "is known." In these places He has made "His abode" and "established . . . his dwelling."

This is great news, for God was under no compulsion to reveal Himself. Anything God has shown us of Himself is pure grace. He has, if you will, opened the cockpit door and let us peer in upon Him.

The good news that God made Himself known "In Judah . . . in Israel . . . in Salem . . . in Zion" of course has another side to it. It means that God had not revealed Himself in this same way in North America, Europe, South Africa or China.

Once while flying into Mongolia I struck up a conversation with a young couple from Ecuador. I asked what brought them to the deserts of Mongolia. Turns out they traveled halfway around the world to observe a solar eclipse. I'm sure it was a remarkable phenomenon, but couldn't you just catch it online? No, it had to be experienced firsthand. And that eclipse was only visible from certain parts of the earth. If you wanted to observe it, you had to go there.

Psalm 76 isn't talking about an eclipse, but a revelation. A revelation that required being in Israel and its capital, Jerusalem. It isn't that God didn't want His self-revelation known and seen in those other places. He made Himself known in a particular place so that those who had experienced it could tell of it to everyone in all the other places of the world.

Today if you want to know God, you must go to Scripture and the one to which it all points: Jesus.

The Bible is a progressive revelation. Creation. Noah. Abraham. Israel. And the record of them is in Scripture. They all point to Jesus. As I have written elsewhere: God chose *one man* (Abraham) through whom He would bring forth *one great nation* (Israel) through which He would bring forth the *one great Savior* (Jesus) in order to demonstrate His glory and extend His grace to *all the peoples of the earth.*[2]

Not only has God revealed Himself in a particular place, but He has done so *in a particular way*. In these very places God "broke the flashing arrows, the shield, the sword, and the weapons of war" (Ps. 76:3).

The God of Abraham, Isaac, Jacob, Moses, David (and the rest of the cast in Scripture's drama) *did* something which revealed Himself. God showed up in time and space in a particular set of circumstances and *acted* to back up His previously given word of revelation.

In a moment we'll examine what those circumstances likely were. But before we do, admit in prayer: "God, I feel like I need You to show up and demonstrate Yourself as the God I read about on the pages of Scripture."

Will He? Should I expect Him to?

You object, "I've prayed that way and God hasn't shown up like this for me!"

No, now see, that's where you're wrong. He has.

The revelation God made in Jerusalem was intended to be, and indeed has been, heralded around the world to all peoples, including you. He revealed Himself to a particular people so that they could tell all people, you among them. God did it in a particular place so that it could be told in every place, including where you live. He gave it to a particular people so it could be told to all peoples, including the people among whom you live.

The oft repeated New Testament expression "it is written" really has the sense of "it stands written." It was written in the past and it stands on record as God's revelation, not only to those who first heard that word, but to all those who can now read it or hear it read—and that includes you.

God has revealed Himself to you and He will hold you to what He's shown you. God has spoken and you are accountable for what He has said. We know this because, not only has God revealed Himself, but . . .

God Has Recompensed Himself

> 4 Glorious are you, more majestic
> than the mountains full of prey.
>
> 5 The stouthearted were stripped of their spoil;
> they sank into sleep;
> all the men of war
> were unable to use their hands.
>
> 6 At your rebuke, O God of Jacob,
> both rider and horse lay stunned.

God defeated a particular foe on a particular day in a particular way. The psalm doesn't tell us specifically when and where this took place and who was involved. Many scholars believe it arose during the days of Isaiah when God delivered Hezekiah and Judah from the hands of the Assyrians.[3] It was such a powerful, divine deliverance that the story is told three different times in the Old Testament (see 2 Kings 18–19; 2 Chron. 32; Isaiah 36–37).

The armies of Sennacherib, king of Assyria, swept across the landscape, devouring every city and village in their path. In time, the worst nightmare of God's people and their king, Hezekiah, came true—the Assyrians encircled Jerusalem as well. The Assyrian envoys taunted them and defamed their God. From a human perspective all hope was lost. Surrender seemed the only path forward. But Hezekiah spotted another course—the way of faith. He humbled himself and called out to God, asking Isaiah the prophet to do the same. Through Isaiah, God returned a word of promise to the penitent king. And under the cover of darkness "the angel of the LORD went out and struck down 185,000 in the camp of the Assyrians. And when people arose early in the morning, behold, these were all dead bodies" (Isa. 37:36).

Yes!, you cry, pumping your fist in triumph. *That's what I need! I need God to show up and smite a few people!*

It's like we're gathering for a fireworks display. We come dragging our lawn chairs, coolers and insect repellent to stake out a spot from which to watch the show.

Be careful, you may get what you ask for. The warning of the prophet Amos still stands:

> Woe to you who desire the day of the LORD!
> Why would you have the day of the LORD?
> It is darkness, and not light,
> as if a man fled from a lion,
> and a bear met him,
> or went into the house and leaned his hand
> against the wall,
> and a serpent bit him.
> Is not the day of the LORD darkness, and not light,
> and gloom with no brightness in it?
> (Amos 5:18–20)

Be assured, God will have the last word.

God will judge *all things*. "I will gather all the nations and bring them down to the Valley of Jehoshaphat. And I will enter into judgment with them there" (Joel 3:2).

God will judge *each one*.

> Then I saw a great white throne and him who was seated on it. From his presence earth and sky fled away, and no place was found for them. And I saw the dead, great and small, standing before the throne, and books were opened. Then another book was opened, which is the book of life. And the dead

> were judged by what was written in the books, according to what they had done. And the sea gave up the dead who were in it, Death and Hades gave up the dead who were in them, and they were judged, *each one of them*, according to what they had done. Then Death and Hades were thrown into the lake of fire. This is the second death, the lake of fire. And if anyone's name was not found written in the book of life, he was thrown into the lake of fire. (Rev. 20:11–15)

So we remember the particulars of God's revelation and of His recompense. But what conclusions or principles should we draw from this? Two, according to the psalmist.

God Rules Over All Opposition

> 7 But you, you are to be feared!
> Who can stand before you
> when once your anger is roused?
>
> 8 From the heavens you uttered judgment;
> the earth feared and was still,
>
> 9 when God arose to establish judgment,
> to save all the humble of the earth. *Selah*

What began with in a particular place—"Judah . . . Israel . . . Salem . . . Zion" (Ps. 76:1, 2)—now is applied to "the earth" to "all the humble of the earth" and to "the kings of the earth" (76:8, 9, 12).

A pattern begins to emerge in what may feel like Asaph's aimless musings. He is now drawing universal principles and applying them to all opposition (not just ancient Assyrians) which stands in the way of God's purposes through His people.

And what conclusion does he reach?

That all who do not yield to God should fear! "But you, you are to be feared!" (Ps. 76:7). Asaph keeps sounding this single note again and again throughout the song:

- "you are to be feared" (76:7)
- "the earth feared" (76:8)
- "him who is to be feared" (76:11)
- "who is to be feared by the kings of the earth" (76:12).

But why? Why should we fear the Lord?

Two great reasons are set before us. The first has to do with God's anger. Asaph asks freely: "Who can stand before you when once your anger is roused?" (76:7).

As you reflect on the nature and attributes of God, if you do not ask "who can stand before" such a being, you need to rethink your understanding of God. You have yet to see Him accurately. Again and again throughout Scripture, when God reveals Himself to a person, he falls down as if dead. Ask Abraham (see Gen. 15:12), Moses (see Exod. 3:6), Joshua (see Josh. 5:14), Daniel (see Dan. 8:18; 10:8, 9), Isaiah (see Isa. 6:5), and Ezekiel (see Ezek. 1:28). Interview Peter (see Luke 5:8) and John (see Rev. 1:17). They'll all tell you the same thing. Down is the only appropriate direction when you see God. The only appropriate question is: "Who can stand before" one so utterly holy?

Indeed, the apostle John reports that . . .

> When he opened the sixth seal, I looked, and behold, there was a great earthquake, and the sun became black as sackcloth, the full moon became like blood, and the stars of the sky fell to the earth as the fig tree sheds its winter fruit when shaken by a gale. The sky vanished like a scroll that is being rolled up, and every mountain and island was removed from its place. Then the kings of the earth and the great ones and the generals and the rich and the powerful, and everyone, slave and free, hid themselves in the caves and among the rocks of the mountains, calling to the mountains and rocks, "Fall on us and hide us from the face of him who is seated on

the throne, and from the wrath of the Lamb, for the great day of their wrath has come, and *who can stand*?" (Rev. 6:12–17)

The second reason for the fear of the Lord has to do with God's judgment.

> 8 From the heavens you uttered judgment;
> the earth feared and was still,
>
> 9 when God arose to establish judgment,
> to save all the humble of the earth.

This God—so ominous and overwhelming in His *anger*—now moves to *act* against those who are found deficient before His blazing holiness!

As Judge, God rules over all opposition that might present itself before Him and those who stand with Him.

But there is more. Not only does God *rule over* all that opposes Him . . .

God Overrules All Opposition

> 10 Surely the wrath of man shall praise you;
> the remnant of wrath you will put on like a belt.
>
> 11 Make your vows to the LORD your God and perform them;
> let all around him bring gifts
> to him who is to be feared,
>
> 12 who cuts off the spirit of princes,
> who is to be feared by the kings of the earth.

Asaph—profoundly awed before this God—is capable only of blurting out: "Surely the wrath of man shall praise you" (Ps. 76:10).

In judgment, God does not merely obliterate all opposition; He tames our defiance and makes it come to nothing.

God turns the energy and enmity of a man's rebellion and causes it to bring about the very thing which it was actively opposing. That which refused to bow in service to God and His purposes is turned back upon itself and made to serve His purposes. That which it sought to stop, it unwittingly brings about. That which meant to defame God, in fact turns out to promote His fame.

God *rules over* all opposition precisely by *overruling* all opposition.

The word translated "praise you" is the same word twice translated as "thanks" at the beginning of the previous psalm (75:1). The point is that each and every expression of rebellion, obstinacy, independence and autonomy ends up bowing down and giving honor, glory, praise and thanksgiving to the God who rules all and overrules all.

A skeptic might demand, *Give me an example!*

No problem.

Consider the case of Pharaoh. Again and again he defied God. To him God replied, "But for this purpose I have raised you up, to show you my power, so that my name may be proclaimed in all the earth" (Exod. 9:16). Again and again God trumped Pharaoh's expressions of sovereignty.

Or take Sennacherib, the king of Assyria, who we considered just moments ago. His defiance may provide the backdrop of this very psalm. He tore through nation after nation. He devastated and subdued countless cities and villages. He marched on Jerusalem, besieged it, threatening to bring it down. In the process, he defied God to do anything to stop him. You now know the outcome of God's nighttime raid on Sennacherib's camp.

Or reflect upon the death of Jesus Christ.

From the moment of His birth, Satan sought to destroy Jesus and derail God's plan (see Matt. 2:16–18). When Jesus did not give way before his temptations in the wilderness, "he departed from him until an opportune time" (Luke 4:13). It was the devil who was behind the Jewish leadership's efforts to kill Jesus (see John 8:44). It was he who put it into the heart of Judas to betray Jesus (see John 13:2). Destroying Jesus before He could destroy him seemed Satan's last, most desperate hope.

Yet the simple fact is that "Jesus, [was] delivered up according to the definite plan and foreknowledge of God" (Acts 2:23). Yes, Jesus was "crucified and killed by the hands of lawless men" (2:23), but God took their lawless rebellion and made it serve His own purposes and undo all the contrary purposes of the evil one.

Or consider the story of God's people in Vietnam. In 1975, when South Vietnam fell to their Communist neighbors to the north, there were an estimated 150,000 Christians in the country. Decades of silence ensued. Faithful believers across the rest of the world prayed for their brothers and sisters, but no sure word of their welfare could be gained. The secrecy and enforced silence of the godless regime locked down the borders. And news of their condition was scarce and spotty at best. Many Vietnamese gave up their lives as the ultimate sacrifice of worship to their Savior. All suffered horribly. But then shortly after the beginning of the new millennium, word began to trickle out of the country. What had been a tiny seed had grown into a mighty oak. Those 150,000 believers had become a vast, strong, vibrant throng of 1.2 million followers of Jesus Christ![4]

The story has been repeated in China, on perhaps an even grander scale. It has been duplicated in Iran for decades now.

Asaph was right: "the remnant of wrath you will put on like a belt" (Ps. 76:10).

God takes the greatest opposition the evil one and his emissaries can throw down and with it He adorns Himself. Like a championship belt, in triumph the Lord wears the hostility of the unbelieving.

Asaph and Paul agree: "And we know that for those who love God all things work together for good, for those who are called according to his purpose" (Rom. 8:28).

Indeed, literally Asaph wrote: "The wraths [plural] of man praise you." Every one of them—every plot, challenge and rebellion—each and every attempt at autonomy and self-rule is overruled by Him who rules over all.

If you're wondering where justice is, if you're reflecting on the wrongs done to you, the injuries inflicted upon those you love, the griefs visited upon you, then consider that not only will they be judged, but they will be made to do service to your King, to His purposes—purposes that will result ultimately in your blessing.

With Joseph, we will one day be able to reply to all who intend harm: "As for you, you meant evil against me, but God meant it for good." (Gen. 50:20).

And, if by chance you're thinking you can avoid the justice of God, think again.

Stop and Ponder

What should I do, given that God both rules over and overrules all opposition?

That depends upon which side of faith in Christ you're standing on.

For the believer, the call is for renewal. *In faith, pledge yourself to God anew.* "Make your vows to the LORD your God and perform them" (Ps. 76:11). That sounds like an Old Testament version of Romans 12:1: "I appeal to you therefore, brothers, by the mercies of God, to present your bodies as a living sacrifice, holy and acceptable to God, which is your spiritual worship."

For the unbeliever, the call is for repentance. *Offer yourself to God in faith.* Asaph calls to you:

> 11 Let all around him bring gifts
> to him who is to be feared,
>
> 12 who cuts off the spirit of princes,
> who is to be feared by the kings of the earth.

By "bring gifts" he does not mean try to buy off God. You know better, for you've already seen the holiness of God and His anger against sin. No, he means gather up the whole of your life and bring it as tribute to your conquering King.

I picture it this way: the interstates and freeways backed up, bumper to bumper as far as the eye can see. They are filled with moving trucks and pickups, semis and trailers, all loaded with the accumulated substance of people's lives. All are streaming toward the throne of God, bent on laying it down at His feet in humble repentance and faith in Jesus' name.

That God of anger and judgment does not back off the line of His holiness or wink at sin. Rather He turned that wrath in judgment against our sins when He placed them upon His own Son as He hung on the cross. There He judged your sin. Humble yourself and receive God's just verdict against your sin—meted out upon Jesus instead of upon you. Lay claim, by faith, to the righteousness of Christ that has—in a reverse motion of grace—been put to your account as a merciful gift.

So What?

God has revealed Himself. And He's shown He will hold us to what He has revealed. God rules over and overrules all that opposes His revealed purposes.

So what should I do in the face of this? The entire psalm echoes a simple message: *The God who has shown Himself to rule over all and to overrule all, deserves and demands your submission.* The God of all deserves and demands your all.

Before you close this chapter take some time to prayerfully submit yourself to God in Jesus' name.

Worship in Action

- Find a quiet place to be alone with God. Open your Bible to the Psalms (Ps. 139 and 145 are good places to begin) and affirm through prayer the greatness and awesomeness of the God who has revealed Himself to you.
- Then begin to declare, by faith, God's sovereign reign over the specific threats that push against your faith and threaten to instill fear in your heart. Name names. Specify issues. This is no time to be vague. Apply God's sovereignty, by faith, to the specific issues that challenge you.
- After you have thoroughly done so, ask God to turn all plots against you and against His will in your life back upon themselves. Ask God to cause them to be self-defeating. Call on God to not only

win in your life, but to bring all opposition into the final outworking of His victory.

- Before you end your time of worship, sit silent and at rest in God's presence. In that place of stillness, thank Him once again. Return to praising His name, His character and His attributes.
- Be at rest as you reengage the world around you.

7

Living a Life of Reflection

Psalm 77

As a rule, when age advances memory retreats. You enter a room, stare, strangely befuddled as to your purpose for coming there; you exit, shaking your head, promising to return when you recall the purpose of your original trip.

Can't relate? Don't worry . . . it's coming! One day you too will curse your fading memory.

While all this is true, we'd be fools to forget those who curse their inability to forget. Closed eyelids are an invitation for replayed scenes of personal tragedy. Silence is a call for sounds of past sorrows to rise to conscious levels.

So we blind ourselves with distractions and blast our ears with noise. Anything to forget!

The capacity to remember is both a blessing and a curse.

I mean not merely that some memories are a blessing and others a curse. True enough. You count the memory of your child's birth as a blessing. If, however, you carry the memory of that child's death, you reckon it a curse.

Clearly this is the case, but I mean more than simply this. I'm suggesting that one singular memory can be, at one and the same time, both a blessing and a curse.

Lift that dusty cardboard box of photos from the top shelf of the closet. Spend an hour shuffling through its contents. How many times do you hold up a single photo and on the one hand say something like, "Oh, remember!" and on the other, "Where have the years gone?" One gives expression to genuine joy, the other to real sadness.

The emotional pendulum swing attached to our memories can be both exhausting and exhilarating. But the fact remains: our capacity for memory is a marvelous gift, given us by God.

The capacity to remember enables us to learn. Memory is the birthplace of progress. Remembrance makes possible the stringing together of one discovery to another and then the connecting of them both to yet a third and, finally, deducing and discovering something from the combination of all of them. All human progress is built upon our God-given capacity to remember.

The ability to remember is a grace given us by our Creator.

As you open to Psalm 77, it is clear that something has stirred Asaph's memory bank. The resulting prayer-song is about living a life of remembrance and reflection.

Note the key words and phrases scattered throughout the psalm:

- "I remember" (77:3)
- "I meditate" (77:3)[1]
- "Let me remember" (77:6)
- "Let me meditate" (77:6)
- "I will remember" (77:11, twice)
- "I will ponder . . . and meditate" (77:12).

Living a life of worship requires living a life of reflection. Worship rises from remembrance. Without memory, worship is condemned to the shallows of the momentary, the fleeting, confined merely to the "now."

If we would worship, we must remember.

Reflection Can Be Painful

However, not far down memory lane you realize reflection can create anguish. See if you can identify the pockmarks of pain in the road of remembering as Asaph begins his prayer.

> 1 I cry aloud to God,
> aloud to God, and he will hear me.
>
> 2 In the day of my trouble I seek the Lord;
> in the night my hand is stretched out without wearying;
> my soul refuses to be comforted.
>
> 3 When I remember God, I moan;
> when I meditate, my spirit faints. *Selah*
>
> 4 You hold my eyelids open;
> I am so troubled that I cannot speak.
>
> 5 I consider the days of old,
> the years long ago.
>
> 6 I said, "Let me remember my song in the night;
> let me meditate in my heart."

Do you see the pain oozing from Asaph's quill?

"I cry aloud to God, aloud to God" (Ps. 77:1) could be more woodenly rendered, "My voice to God, and I cry, my voice to God!" And the word rendered "cry" is freighted with a sense of volume and emotion. It is a ringing cry in the spirit of: "God! Where are You?" The repetition of "aloud" makes emphatic a pain too powerful to remain inaudible.

All this arises from "the day of my trouble" (77:2). The picture is of being pressed in upon, squeezed, constrained and constricted—and this by the pressure of memories flooding in from the past.

The anguish came upon Asaph "in the night" (Ps. 77:2, 6). Sleep too often flees under threats of recollection.

His mind writhed between the rock of past memories and the hard place of present longings.

Asaph confessed, "my hand is stretched out without wearying" (77:2). Were you at 3:00 a.m. to suddenly flip on the light in his room, you'd find his eyes open, tears streaming down his cheeks, a hand reaching toward heaven as he cries, "God! God! Where are You?"

"I moan" (77:3), says Asaph. The word had the idea of murmuring, growling or even a roar.[2] There is in it the idea of crying aloud in a rage. It can describe a tumult or uproar.[3] And what creates this reaction? Reflection upon God!

Sometimes you moan from something that has been *added* to your life—pain. Like a person who awakens in the emergency room. At other times you moan because something seems to have been *taken* from your life. The emotional mess arises from loss. Like a person sitting in an emotional stupor at the funeral home, suddenly bereft of a loved one.

In all this, the psalmist discloses, "my spirit faints" (77:3). Strength flags and fails. This is the swimmer struggling to make it to shore. There comes that moment of clarity when it dawns upon you that the distance to be covered and the strength that remains are not equal. You've not yet drowned, but it won't be long.

Yet, God, "you hold my eyelids open" (77:4). There is no relief, even in sleep. A common sign of depression is the inability to get out of bed—the seeming requirement of inordinate amounts of sleep. The Lord of all memories seems to prop your eyelids open and withhold the "peace" that comes with at least checking out for a while. He seems to demand your full and constant attention to what you're suffering.

"I am so troubled that I cannot speak" (Ps. 77:4). We've cycled from desperate screams in verse 1 to speechlessness in verse 4; from ringing cries to deafening silence.

Robert Duvall's character in the film *Get Low*[5] powerfully depicts the painful powers of memory. Based on a true story, Felix Bush, portrayed by Duvall, is a hermit who has lived in self-imposed isolation for forty years. The residents of the surrounding counties have filled those four decades with salacious rumors and tales of atrocities committed. The accounts grow more fearsome during their cycles through the rumor mill. Urged on by the recent death of an old acquaintance, Bush determines to hold his own funeral . . . prior to his decease. The advertised purpose of his odd pre-death funeral is for the spiteful, gossiping neighbors to all turn out and tell their stories of Felix. This is the draw. But his ultimate purpose is to tell his story—the true story, to unleash memories that have held him prisoner these many years.

When finally the day dawns, crowds pour in (in real life some ten thousand people showed up for Felix's pre-decease funeral). Eventually, the reclusive Bush makes his way to the microphone where he divulges the awful, sinful choices he made as a young man—shameful choices which cost someone he loved her life. He opens the long-locked-down vault in his memory bank; festering, putrid pain oozes. And, in the end, he asks them to forgive him.

To his surprise, his heart is set free. But not even this freedom can recapture decades of life lost to the haunting specter of his memories.

What caused the psalmist such anguish?

Surprisingly, it was not negative memories. It was thoughts of God—"When I remember God" (Ps. 77:3)—and the memories of what He had done and the grace He extended in the past—"I consider the days of old, the years long ago" (77:5), "your wonders of old" (77:11)! It was memories of God's goodness that caused such anguish.

Are you haunted not by bad memories, but by good ones? What are these memories?

- *"You know, God used to ________."*
- *"Do you remember when God ________?"*
- *"Remember when we would pray and then God would ________?"*
- *"Did you ever read about the time God ________?"*

The church in America is haunted by good memories. Certainly we have some bad ones as well, but the knowledge of how things once were with God and the awareness that we simply aren't living there anymore can be a heavy burden. Reading the historical accounts of the sinner-converting, life-transforming, family-saving power of the simple gospel message spoken in sincerity can leave one wondering what ossifying deadness has crept over our hearts in these latter years. The reading of the Bible would break hard hearts, repentance would result, confession of sin would flow, lives would be restored, marriages saved.

Too many churches are haunted by good memories—tales of the glory years, memories of what once was, reflections of how God once revealed His hand in their midst. Sometimes it hurts to remember the good times.

Perhaps that's true in your own personal relationship to God as well. "We have heard it with our ears, O God; our ancestors have told us what you did in their days, in days long ago" (Ps. 44:1, NIV).

We have memories, wonderful memories! But they haunt us because they remind us of a grace that was real, life change that was actual, transforming power that was active. Sadly, in our day, it seems that such grace and power reside only in our memory banks and historical archives.

The psalmist cries, "Let me remember my song in the night" (77:6)! *I used to have a song I could pull out in the dark of the night and sing in praise to God. Heaviness of spirit was sent packing when brought before the throne of God.*

What happened to that song?

What does this kind of reflection produce? Not only anguish, but questions! Five of them to be exact:

> 7 Will the Lord spurn forever,
> and never again be favorable?
>
> 8 Has his steadfast love forever ceased?
> Are his promises at an end for all time?
>
> 9 Has God forgotten to be gracious?
> Has he in anger shut up his compassion?

The answer? In all five cases the expected answer is a resounding "No!" God cannot change. He can never renege on a promise. He is faithful and true.

You know that—somewhere deep in your heart. You've known it for a long time. There was a day you would have never even considered asking the questions, but the collision of present realities and remembrances of a blessed past have introduced painful questions to your heart.

Are you frightened by the very questions you find yourself asking?

Worship—real, authentic, genuine worship—is not destroyed by this kind of honesty. It actually requires it.

So we come to realize that while reflection can indeed be painful, it can also be worshipful. This is precisely what the latter half of Asaph's prayer reveals.

Reflection Can Be Worshipful

So what is one to do in the face of these wonderful, painful memories?

Here is the pivot upon which the entire prayer turns:

> 10 Then I said, "I will appeal to this,
> to the years of the right hand of the Most High."

Here is how our memory-work moves us from pain to praise, from grief to worship.

But this is a difficult verse to translate. Let's take just a moment, therefore, to highlight what is at play.

The text of the English Standard Version and the alternate translation provided in the margin reveal the basic issues. Again, the text reads: "Then I said, 'I will appeal to this, to the years of the right hand of the Most High.'" The issues revolve around these two words—*appeal* and *years*. The translation offered in the margin reveals this very thing: "This is my *grief*: that the right hand of the Most High has *changed*." It won't take you long to discover that English translations vary between these options.

What is behind all this? In most any language a given word may have a range of meanings. It is true in Hebrew, as in English. For example, "John" may refer to a person or to a toilet. Or take the word "bank." Sometimes it refers to the earthen edge of a river and in other situations to a financial institution. A "bow" may be something used with a violin or an arrow, a decorative item atop a gift or a tie worn with a dress shirt. You only know which meaning is the intended one by the context in which it is employed.

So it is here. One Hebrew word can mean either "appeal" or "grief" and the other "years" or "changed."

How do we know which means what in this particular case? The question is not merely academic, for this line is the pivot on which the entire psalm turns.[5] I suggest that the English Standard Version has rendered it correctly.

The Hebrew word translated "years" (or "changed") has just been translated "years" in verse 5. We know that "years" is the correct translation in verse 5 because it is paralleled to "the days of" (a reference to a segment of time). A word used a second time in so brief a space would tend to be used in a similar sense. So it seems safe to say "years" is the correct translation here.

So?

This means the psalmist is looking back on his experience with God. He is reviewing God's dealings with him over the course of time—God's grace, His saving acts, specific instances when God came through.

What about the other word? Should it be translated "appeal" or "grief"?

If it means "appeal" then we have the expression of the psalmist's prayer. He is praying something like this: "I am looking back upon the record of Your dealings with me ('the years of the right hand of the Most High'), O God. And, despite the fact that it seems You have been handling my present crisis contrary to Your normal, gracious way, I am making my prayer, my appeal to You on this basis—that You, O God, have a record of being faithful and true to Your word, good and gracious to me, moving in power on behalf of Your people and keeping Your promises. God, You have been so good in the past. Be gracious to me once again." This is a way of reasoning confirmed elsewhere in the Bible.

If, on the other hand, the word means "grief," the psalmist is saying, "I reflect upon the record of Your gracious and powerful dealings with me in the past and I try to make sense of Your present manner with me. What's changed, O God? *You* seem to have changed. Where is Your faithfulness, Your grace, Your mercy, Your kindness which I have known in the past? Why do You not deal with me thus now?"

So which is it? Appeal or grief?

The psalm itself tells us it is *both*! The review of God's past dealings with him has produced "grief," as the first half of the psalm has revealed (Ps. 77:1–9). But those same remembrances are about to bring hope—hope that moves the psalmist to make his fresh "appeal" to God in the latter part of the psalm (77:11–20).

Odd, isn't it, that the same memories that bring pain can also bring joy? The same review of God's past dealings that produced "grief" (77:1–9) now brings forth hope ("appeal," 77:11–20)! The same remembrances that in one instance lead to groaning, moaning, crying and screaming, can also lead to worship, prayer, song and hope.

What makes the difference? What tips the scale of our memories in either the direction of grief or of worshipful hope?

The difference is revealed in a little phrase repeated in rapid succession: "I will" (77:10, 11, 12).

"I will" *what?*

I will make the decision to take my eyes off of my present, apparent lack (and the pain it creates) and put my eyes back on *You*, O God!

- "*I will appeal*" to Your record of faithfulness, O God (77:10).
- "*I will remember* the deeds" You have done (77:11).
- "*I will remember* your wonders of old" (77:11).
- "*I will ponder* all your work, and meditate on your mighty deeds" (77:12).

Same action; different object. I'm still exercising my memory bank. But this time I'm remembering God instead of my list of grievances. The same memory, but a different perspective. What once was hurt, now is hope.

There are times in our journey with God when we must honestly confess to God, "I remember, O God, when we had better days together. I remember Your acts of grace, Your moving in power on my behalf. And I have to tell You, it pains me deeply that You seem to have changed. But *I will* set my eyes upon You, O God. My reality will not be determined by my feelings, nor by the circumstances that feed my feelings. My reality is determined by You, God. *I will* worship You. *I will* hope in You."

A determination to worship God, regardless of circumstance or feeling unleashes awesome power to change your perspective.

Check the pronouns in the psalm. In the first half of the psalm (see 77:1–9) the pronouns "I," "me" and "my" are used twenty times. Yes, he is remembering what God has done, but he is doing it primarily from the angle of self-interest. In the latter half of the psalm (see Ps. 77:11–20), once you take out those "I will" statements, the personal pronouns don't appear even once. Something has changed, profoundly so. Clearly there is grief in becoming too self-focused.

Check also the references to God. In the first half of the psalm, God is mentioned—whether by name, title or pronoun—twelve times. Not even close to as many times as the psalmist was talking about himself. But in the second half, God is referenced twenty-four times![6]

The continental divide between pain and worship runs along the ridgeline of "I will." *I will focus on God. I have made up my mind; I will worship God in the midst of the mess.*

Doesn't this sound a bit like covenant language? Is there not an echo in all of this that sounds a great deal like marriage vows? There you are, standing before one another in a brilliantly beautiful, perfectly romantic setting, filled with positive emotions and saying to one another "I will." You do so *then* so that in future days, in other circumstances and with other kinds of feelings, you will have already determined—"I will." It was settled long ago; come what may, "I will."

That is exactly what this is—wedding ourselves to God as His worshipers.

Reflecting helps us worship God. When I take up the memories and focus upon God rather than upon what I feel, what do I find?

I find that I remember God's *actions*.

> 11 I will remember the deeds of the LORD;
> yes, I will remember your wonders of old.
>
> 12 I will ponder all your work,
> and meditate on your mighty deeds.

God has acted powerfully, savingly, personally, graciously. I remember that God is a God of gracious power.

I find that I remember God's *nature* (Ps. 77:13–15). By nature God is unique:

> 13 Your way, O God, is holy.
> What god is great like our God?

Being "holy" can refer to purity, but its more basic idea is that of being "other." God is completely unlike, different from anything we know. God is love, but love of a stripe and variety that makes the best of earth's loves but a faint whisper of His real love. God is wise, but wise in a way and from a position and with a perspective that makes any earthly, human wisdom sound hollow. God has a plan, and it isn't the one I dreamed up. According to His own unique love, wisdom and plan, God acts and moves and allows and sends and resources. Little wonder I end up confused at times!

God is *awesome.*

> 14 You are the God who works wonders;
> you have made known your might among the peoples.

God is powerful, *all*-powerful. He is the *Al*mighty. He harnesses His power in the reins of His grace. At the impulse of His will (not my whims), He unleashes it for good upon His children.

God is *loving.*

> 15 You with your arm redeemed your people,
> the children of Jacob and Joseph.

In His holy love God "redeemed" the Israelites. He bought them out of bondage and for Himself. Where did He most clearly do this? At the Red Sea.

> 16 When the waters saw you, O God,
> when the waters saw you, they were afraid;
> indeed, the deep trembled.

17 The clouds poured out water;
the skies gave forth thunder;
your arrows flashed on every side.

18 The crash of your thunder was in the whirlwind;
your lightnings lighted up the world;
the earth trembled and shook.

19 Your way was through the sea,
your path through the great waters;
yet your footprints were unseen.

Then what did God do?

He brought His unique wisdom, immeasurable power and awesome love together to shepherd His people through the wilderness to the Promised Land.

20 You led your people like a flock
by the hand of Moses and Aaron.

Did you catch that? "*You* led Your people." God was their Shepherd. He accomplished it "by the hand of Moses and Aaron," but the Lord was their Shepherd.

From foreign slavery, through waters over their heads, across burning wastelands, to Mount Sinai and then through the wilderness for forty years—God shepherded His people. Again and again they thought, "God has abandoned us!" But if they could have lifted their heads and gained the perspective that often comes only with the passage of time, they would have confessed—even in the moment, even in the pain, even in the panic—God has not abandoned us! God is tending us like a flock.

He did so through human instruments—"Moses and Aaron." They were temporary shepherds, for a season, for certain people who found themselves in a certain place at a certain time in a certain set of circumstances.

So what good is this to you?

The good news is that the Lord was the Shepherd; Moses and Aaron were His temporary undershepherds. That same Shepherd eventually took on a human body and came to earth. He said, "I am the good shepherd. The good shepherd lays down his life for the sheep. I am the good shepherd. I know my own and my own know me" (John 10:11, 14).

It's not that Jesus *was* the Good Shepherd; He *is* the Good Shepherd—because He not only laid down His life for the sheep at the cross, but He is alive forevermore through resurrection from the dead. Jesus is not temporary. He is not just for a season. He is not just for a certain people, in a certain place, at a certain time or in a certain set of circumstances. He will be the Good Shepherd of your life, as you wed yourself to Him with your "I will!" of faith.

Suppose you make the journey from ringing cries full of pain to the submissive "I will!" of worship—the journey from verse 1 to verse 20. Have your circumstances changed?

No.

Has God changed?

No.

But have *you* changed?

Yes.

Has your *perspective* changed?

Yes.

Has your *experience* in the midst of your circumstances changed?

Yes! Gloriously, wonderfully, yes!

Is everything better?

No.

Are *things* better?

Yes, because remembrance and reflection have led me to worship—and worship has drawn me again to God!

As we bring this chapter to a close, allow me to draw upon the experiences of Robertson McQuilkin, a Christian leader and longtime president of Columbia International University. As you'll see, he is a man who knows something about both pain and worship.

> I arrived just as my sister, Virginia, was lifted from the ambulance, strapped to a metal stretcher. When she saw me, her greeting was simply, "God has abandoned me." Maybe you'd feel that way, too, if your husband had died an agonizing death of cancer less than a year before and this was your second car accident in that same year—the one you knew intuitively would end your driving forever. But her voice was flat—no wail of self-pity or angry accusations against God. It wasn't the first time my sister had felt abandoned by God. Actually, she's felt that way periodically over the past 20 years since Margie, her only daughter and the joy of her life, was brutally killed. It didn't help that her murderer had killed before and had just been released from prison on the advice of a court-appointed psychiatrist. It didn't make sense that a young woman who loved God and people so intensely should be snuffed out by a madman. Perhaps God abandoned her too! . . .
>
> [My wife] Muriel was a chain worrier. One stormy night she was totally stressed out about her three teenagers who were out in the fringes of the hurricane. She was just as distraught over the last two when the first arrived in good cheer, unscathed, and still immobilized by fear for the third after the second appeared. As she writhed in an agony of worry on her bed, harassing the Lord with her unbelief, he seemed to say to her, *Do you want to spend the rest of your life living like this?* Startled, she cried out, "Oh no, Lord! I truly don't. Please deliver me!" And, as she never tired of testifying, he did. In an instant. For most of us it takes a bit of growing, but not for Muriel. She

just quit once she got focused on who God really is. . . .

A few years later, the ministry for which I was responsible was not doing well, not doing well at all. I cried out to God for deliverance and victory but it seemed my prayers weren't getting through. So I went out on the mountainside—perhaps with no ceiling those prayers would rise higher! But still the line was dead. Then a thought broke through: *Try praise.* I was so out of practice in praise, I ran out of thanksgivings and praise in five minutes. But my soul was uncaged, and I discovered that *the weary spirit rises on the wings of praise.* And no wonder—to focus on God sets me free from my own finitudes and fallenness. . . .

My beloved [wife] was being taken from me little by little in the 80s, and then the blow fell: my eldest son was killed in a tragic diving accident. All accidental deaths are tragic, no doubt, but this one was so preventable. Two years later I resigned the presidency of Columbia International University to care for my beloved, leaving my life's work at its peak. I was numb under the blows of life. . . .

This was a call to do what I learned early in ministry—off to a mountain hideaway to be alone with God. There, as I focused again on him, I discovered that indeed the heavy heart lifts on the wings of praise.[7]

Worship in Action

- Find a place where you can not only be alone with God for a protracted period of time, but where you can speak your prayers audibly, without concern for who might hear.
- Begin by submitting yourself afresh to the Lord in definite prayer. Then ask God to search your heart and bring to your mind the most painful memories of your life. Write them down.
- When ready, begin praying through those memories, describing them to God, allowing the raw, authentic emotions to become a genuine part of your words to God. Pray aloud. Articulate your thoughts and emotions to God.
- What questions do these memories and their emotions leave you with? Still consciously in God's presence, write them down. Take your time; don't rush.
- Then, even if it seems inappropriate or you are embarrassed to do so, honestly tell God of the questions these memories leave you with.
- The goal is not that you receive answers that entirely satisfy you. The point is that, by authentically sharing your heart, you invite God into those events, the memories and emotions they create and the questions that are left in their wake.

- Tell God you would like to understand, but leave to Him your desire for answers to your questions.
- Now transition in your prayers to a season of giving thanks to God for the times He has demonstrated His grace, power and love in your life. Ask Him to aid you here as well, bringing to your memory the things He has done on your behalf.
- Let these memories become audible prayers of thanksgiving, praise and worship. Take your time. Don't cut this short. Linger until your heart is refreshed and your spirit at rest once again in who God is and in His shepherding care.

8

Living a Life of Faithfulness

Psalm 78

Just "going to worship" isn't enough. It's too convenient, too cubbyholed, too compartmentalized. God will not be so conveniently tucked away and tamed.

Life (all of it!) as worship is His right and demand.

If we are to make that transition from the one to the other, we must lift our eyes, see further and think beyond ourselves. We must look both backward and forward—to where we've come from, but also to those who will come after us. Life as worship requires living beyond yourself.

Psalm 78 aids us here,[1] by putting our heads on a swivel and bidding us to *review the past to change the present and to give hope for the future.*

Mark it well, for this is the road map for the journey ahead—not only to Psalm 78, but to living life as worship to the Lord. Worship is about more than singing songs of worship, praying prayers, giving offerings and listening to sermons. If you don't live life every day as worship, the activities of Sunday morning are largely meaningless.

The psalmist tips his hand right up front, telling us what is at stake. Watch for three key words that unlock the mystery of living a life of faithfulness as worship. Mark these words:

fathers, children and *generation*. And remember, the psalmist uses these three words to help us review the past so we can change the present and, therefore, have hope for the future.

> 1 Give ear, O my people, to my teaching;
> incline your ears to the words of my mouth!
>
> 2 I will open my mouth in a parable;
> I will utter dark sayings from of old,
>
> 3 things that we have heard and known,
> that our *fathers* have told us.
>
> 4 We will not hide them from their *children*,
> but tell to the coming *generation*
> the glorious deeds of the LORD, and his might,
> and the wonders that he has done.
>
> 5 He established a testimony in Jacob
> and appointed a law in Israel,
> which he commanded our *fathers*
> to teach to their *children*,
>
> 6 that the next *generation* might know them,
> the *children* yet unborn,
> and arise and tell them to their *children*,
>
> 7 so that they should set their hope in God
> and not forget the works of God,
> but keep his commandments;
>
> 8 and that they should not be like their *fathers*,
> a stubborn and rebellious *generation*,
> a *generation* whose heart was not steadfast,
> whose spirit was *not faithful to God*.

Triangulate fathers, children and generations and you have the psalmist's center—faithfulness (see Ps. 78:8). A glance in the rearview mirror too often reveals fathers who have not been faithful. Thus, the present state of things is not as God desires. And of course this jeopardizes the future, robbing us of hope.

Asaph lived so contagiously that his influence spanned multiple generations—in fact, over half a millennium! Faithfulness is required to live so infectiously that one generation after another carries the current of faith forward to the next.

Real People Retailing God

The psalmist, by necessity, speaks in concrete terms of real people as he first looks backward toward those who have gone before, the fathers of his people. Specifically, he makes mention of Ephraim (see Ps. 78:9).

Ephraim?

Sit tight while I set the stage.

Ephraim was one of Joseph's two sons, the other being Manasseh. These boys were adopted by their grandfather, Jacob, and placed in the position of firstborn among the sons of Jacob—taking the place of his firstborn, but unfaithful, son Reuben (see Gen. 48:8-20). Through the centuries, Ephraim became the strongest of the tribes that made up the northern kingdom of Israel. Sometimes, as in this case, the entire northern kingdom was referred to simply as Ephraim. After Solomon's death, the ten northern tribes rebelled against Solomon's son Rehoboam, withdrawing to establish their own kingdom to the north (leaving the tribes of Judah and Benjamin to form the southern kingdom). It didn't take them long to realize that if their citizens regularly crossed the border to worship in Jerusalem it would destabilize their nation. So they set up their own system of worship, their own worship center, an alternate priesthood and a man-commissioned altar (see 1 Kings 12:25–33). As such Ephraim (the northern kingdom) represented a people who had rejected God and His ways.

They wanted God on their terms, worship in their way. They determined to worship at their own convenience—where they wished, when they wished.

In this, they cast a shadow that has become the substance of our consumer-oriented, western Christian culture where almost everything is bent toward the will of the worshiper, rather than toward the one to be worshiped. Worship in such a context becomes a celebration, not of the sovereignty of God, but the sovereignty of the worshiper. They come before God to allow Him a chance to meet their needs, to invite Him to bow to their troubles and to give Him an opportunity to abandon His plans and join them in theirs.

This is nothing short of *the retailing of God!*

Our word "retail" comes from the Old French. The prefix *re-* means "back," while *tail* means "to cut" or "to trim." The resulting combination came to describe selling in small quantities. In time it described "a piece cut off, shred, scrap, paring."[2]

That is precisely what's left after self-defined, self-directed worship—shreds and scraps of God. There is something of God here, but it is bits and pieces sewn together into a quilt of worship after a pattern of one's own making. Such worship constructs a patchwork, piecemeal deity, fit neither to command our allegiance nor meet our needs.

God judges such people unfaithful. His verdict is their "heart was not steadfast" and their "spirit was not faithful to God" (Ps. 78:8). Indeed, the "Ephraimites . . . did not keep God's covenant, but refused to walk according to his law. They forgot his works and the wonders that he had shown them" (78:9–11). By the end of the psalm, he will tell us, "He rejected the tent of Joseph; he did not choose the tribe of Ephraim" (78:67).

We must review the past, but a mere history lesson is not our goal. We've already seen some painful reflections of what passes for worship in our own day. That is appropriate, for "these things happened to them as an example [the past], but they were written down for our instruction [the present], on whom the end of the ages has come [the future]" (1 Cor. 10:11).

This is about Ephraim, but it is also about me!

Remember: the psalm reviews the past to change the present so we can have hope for the future. As we do just that, we recall that this is about faithfulness—and not just Ephraim's, but mine as well.

Okay, but what's at stake? Why should I care?

Honest questions. Here's a candid answer: *If fathers are unfaithful, children will wander. If children wander, whole generations will be lost!*

A Line of Grace

Think of it this way. Suppose you came upon a perfectly straight line. And further suppose that you then tried to draw a line perfectly parallel to it. Let's say that the first line is ten feet in length. Your first attempt is, say, an inch long.

Is your line parallel to the other?

As you eyeball it, it appears parallel.

You've done your best. But how do you know if it's really parallel?

You extend it further. You lengthen it from one inch to one foot, from one foot to five feet . . . and on to ten.

Quickly you realize that a microvariation at the one inch mark becomes a more serious deviation at ten feet. And what if the two lines were extended to ten miles?

You've got yourself an unbridgeable gulf.

In this new light, then, listen again.

> 8 they should not be like their *fathers*,
> a stubborn and rebellious *generation*,
> a *generation* whose heart was *not steadfast*,
> whose spirit was *not faithful to God*.

God laid down a line of grace. He blessed them; He called them. They responded, but it was not with a parallel life. They wanted something of God in their lives, but they wanted God on their terms. They didn't want to be a godless people, but neither did they want an entirely God-defined life. They wanted God in a box of their construction.

Over the course of a lifetime, with the passing of a generation, in the succession of multiple generations, what do you have?

A broad, nearly insurmountable chasm between the line of God's grace and the line of "worship" we've laid down.

This is precisely what happened in Israel's history. It came after the remarkable, often miraculous, provisions God poured out during the days of Moses. It followed the faithful leadership of Joshua which settled the people in the Promised Land. Toward the end of his life, Joshua challenged the people: "Choose this day whom you will serve, whether the gods your fathers served in the region beyond the River, or the gods of the Amorites in whose land you dwell. But as for me and my house, we will serve the LORD" (Josh. 24:15).

Noting the straight line of God's constant grace, Joshua said, "You've got to draw your line of response to this grace. Draw it as you will. But I and my family are laying down a line of faithfulness that runs parallel to God's goodness to us!"

It was not long, however, after Joshua's challenge that the ancient historian recorded these words: "And all that generation also were gathered to their fathers. And there arose another generation after them who did not know the LORD or the work that he had done for Israel" (Judg. 2:10).

Ask yourself: *What's at stake in my response to God?*

God extends His grace, love and mercy. He does it faithfully, fully, superabundantly. He has done it ultimately in Jesus Christ—God become man to rescue us from the unbridgeable gulf created by our sin. Though fully God, Jesus lived in a very human body, took on a human nature and spent a lifetime on our turf. Having negotiated His course through this world without sinning, He went to the cross to pay for ours.

God gives. God lays down the line of His grace.

We each one make our response to that line of grace. Some try to ignore Him; others consciously reject Him—in either case, drawing a bold, perpendicular line!

But many, especially those of you reading this book, desire to respond to that grace. You want God in your life. You lay down a line of response that reflects His grace.

Is it parallel? Is it commensurate to the grace extended to us through Jesus Christ?

For starters, "Oh yes! I want to go with Jesus! I believe! I will follow!"

As a start, it looks like a good line, a parallel line. But extended over a series of months and years, how does that line measure up? A lifetime later, where are you in comparison with the line of God's grace?

"Well, I'm still in the vicinity. If I want to get back to it, I know where to find it."

Generational Transfer

But here's what happens. Not only over the course of a lifetime do the two lines reveal the truth, but also, and even more so, over the course of generational transfer.

So you respond to Jesus and tell Him you'll be His follower. You begin well enough. But extended out over a series of decades, down through the years, culminating at the time of your death—what does a lifetime reveal? Where does that leave you twenty, thirty, forty years down the line?

Suppose that line of grace includes a family. Where do they begin their own response to the line of God's grace?

We hope they'll go right back to Jesus Himself. Indeed, they need to respond personally to Him.

The reality, however, is that in many ways they begin their line where yours leaves off. They start where they've seen you live your response to God. A response that now, extended over a series of years, may not be all that close to the actual line of grace in the gospel.

The children begin where they saw dad living his life. Then they—over a lifetime—lay down their line of response. Calculate in the variation of their line from their starting point. Where do they leave the legacy at the end of their days? And another generation picks up from there. Add more of the same over another generation.

Multiply all of this over several generations—by now you can't even see the original line of grace!

Why has God made your faithfulness so vital to a life of worship? Because *if fathers are unfaithful, children will wander. If children wander, whole generations will be lost!*

If you depart this life today, what spiritual legacy will you leave to your family? What have you demonstrated to them about living life as worship? When they all gather for the funeral, where will your line of response—as demonstrated by the example of your life—be in relationship to God's line of grace through Jesus Christ?

This is not simply about how we behave ourselves on Sundays, but also in the moments and minutes of life throughout each week. This gets not only at our "worship," but at our words; not just at our hymnbooks, but at our checkbooks; not merely in one hour each weekend, but also in all the hours between our weekends.

Observe how the psalmist demonstrates this for us throughout his prayer. This is the second longest psalm in the entire Psalter, so I'm not going to reproduce every word here. Rather, I'm going to set before you the key words. In fact, I want you to watch for two things—the subjects and the verbs—for they tell the tale of unfaithfulness.

In fact, what I want you to do is to read these lines just as you would watch a tennis match. Just as your head swings from left to right, right to left during a great volley, watch the back and forth movement of God's initiative and the people's response.

Ready? Here we go. God served up grace extended to His people.

> 12 In the sight of their fathers he performed wonders . . .
>
> 13 He divided the sea and let them pass through it,
> and made the waters stand like a heap . . . .
>
> 14 he led them . . .
>
> 15 He split rocks . . .
> and gave them drink . . .
>
> 16 He made streams come out of the rock
> and caused waters to flow down like rivers.

Now watch their response.

> 17 Yet they sinned still more against him . . .
>
> 18 They tested God . . .
>
> 19 They spoke against God . . .

God's response?

> 21 Therefore, when the LORD heard, he was full of wrath . . .
> his anger rose against Israel,
>
> 22 because they did not believe in God
> and did not trust his saving power.
>
> 23 Yet he commanded the skies above
> and opened the doors of heaven,
>
> 24 and he rained down on them manna to eat
> and gave them the grain of heaven
>
> 25 . . . he sent them food in abundance.
>
> 27 he rained meat on them . . .
>
> 29 And they ate and were well filled,
> for he gave them what they craved.

Now again, their response.

> 32 In spite of all this, they still sinned;
> despite his wonders, they did not believe.

And God's response?

> 33 So he made their days vanish like a breath,
> and their years in terror.

Wow! Discipline! How did that change things?

> 34 When he killed them, they sought him;
> they repented and sought God earnestly.

35 They remembered that God was their rock,
the Most High God their redeemer.

Ah, but don't get too excited, for this was all just hypocrisy.

36 But they flattered him with their mouths;
they lied to him with their tongues.

37 Their heart was not steadfast toward him;
they were not faithful [there's our theme!] to his covenant.

Dizzy yet? Hang on!

In the face of their hypocrisy and unfaithfulness, what did God do?

38 Yet he, being compassionate,
atoned for their iniquity
and did not destroy them;
he restrained his anger often
and did not stir up all his wrath.

39 He remembered that they were but flesh,
a wind that passes and comes not again.

Now how did the people respond?

40 How often they rebelled against him in the wilderness
and grieved him in the desert!

41 They tested God again and again
and provoked the Holy One of Israel.
42 They did not remember [recall the danger of forgeting the past!] . . .

43 when he performed his signs in Egypt
and his marvels . . .

44 He turned . . .

45 He sent . . .

46 He gave . . .

47 He destroyed . . .

48 He gave over . . .

49 He let loose . . .

50 He made a path . . .

51 He struck down . . .

52 Then he led out his people like sheep
and guided them in the wilderness like a flock.

53 He led them in safety . . .

54 And he brought them to his holy land . . .

55 He drove out nations . . .
he apportioned them for a possession . . .

56 Yet they tested and rebelled against the Most High God
and did not keep his testimonies,

57 but turned away and acted treacherously like their fathers.

It's verifiable from history: *If fathers are unfaithful, children will wander. If children wander, whole generations will be lost!*

When this inviolable process unfolds, how does God feel?

59 When God heard, he was full of wrath,
and he utterly rejected Israel [who had been raised up to proclaim his praises].

60 He forsook his dwelling at Shiloh,
the tent where he dwelt among mankind [where they were to worship him!],

61 and delivered his power [i.e., the ark, the centerpiece of their worship] to captivity,
his glory to the hand of the foe.

62 He gave his people [who failed to respond with lives
of worship] over to the sword
and vented his wrath on his heritage.

63 Fire devoured their young men,
and their young women had no marriage song
[they paid the price for the previous generations' failures of faithfulness].

64 Their priests [those appointed to lead their worship]
fell by the sword,
and their widows made no lamentation.

What you observe like a tennis match—back and forth, serve and volley—is the record of divine faithfulness and human unfaithfulness.

God lays down a line of grace. We lay down a life of response.

A life of worship begins when we realize that faithfulness is not measured merely by our initial response to the news of God's grace in Christ, but by the ongoing life of faithful obedience that issues from that response.

I've also looked into the history of our English word faithfulness. Going back to the early sixteenth century it meant "true to the facts."[3]

Honestly ask and answer this question: Is my life true to the facts of God's grace? Is the line of my life's response true to the facts of God's line of goodness extended to me through Jesus Christ?

Faithfulness is measured over a lifetime by an obedient, submissive, worshipful, whole-life response to the facts of God's grace. Unfaithfulness is drawn with the broad chalk of a life askew of the facts.

God's Ultimate Response

Does this volley of grace and unfaithfulness go on unendingly? How does God respond to perpetual unfaithfulness? What's His response to generational unfaithfulness?

The answer is right here in Psalm 78. And the answer begins where we began—talking about the unfaithful northern kingdom of Israel (Ephraim). What we find is that God responds to congenital unfaithfulness by acting both negatively and positively.

First, the negative response.

> 67 He rejected the tent of Joseph;
> he did not choose the tribe of Ephraim.

That is grace withdrawn.

Huh? What? No, wait! That can't be right. The story can't end like that!

Sorry, but eventually, God simply passes by the one who remains stubbornly unfaithful in the face of grace. God has offered, called, given, extended, waited and been patient. Yet eventually, He pulls back His hand and, with it, the offer of His grace.

A while back I found myself in a meeting where I was introduced to a number of people with whom I was not acquainted. In one instance, I extended my hand as I greeted the individual and, just as I did so, the person looked away. I was left hanging in that awkward moment when you've clearly offered your hand and the person just as clearly disregards you.

Awkward! What are you supposed to do with your extended hand?

Sometimes you try to keep the motion moving upward and make it look like you were actually reaching for something else or raising your hand to smooth your hair. Nobody buys it, but you'll try almost anything to avoid the awkwardness of being left hanging.

I don't know what got into me on this occasion, but, despite the embarrassment of the moment, I decided to try something. I just left my hand out there, extended toward the person—making it painfully obvious that they'd disregarded me. I kept it there, extended toward them. The people immediately around me stared uneasily. The person to whom I'd been introduced had become preoccupied with looking off in the other direction.

And there we were.

Eventually, the individual glanced back and saw my extended arm, my hand still open, offering a handshake of welcome. He was taken aback; the embarrassment registered on his face. He tried to make the best of it, passively taking my hand with a limp grip, and got the social niceties over with as quickly as possible.

I know. I'm weird.

But here's the question I had to ask myself: How long would I have remained in that uneasy position? How long are you willing to be rebuffed, embarrassed and turned away socially? I kept it up for several seconds longer than most would. But I doubt I'd have still been there five minutes later. Forget about an hour or the next day!

At some point, the offer of my extended hand would be withdrawn.

God's offer of grace will not last forever. As patient as He is (see 2 Pet. 3:8–9), God's offer of grace through Jesus Christ is not without end. For those who respond in repentant faith and obedience, that grace will never be overcome and will never run out. But the offer of that inexhaustible grace will eventually be withdrawn.

Death may come. Christ will return. Through repeated rejection of His mercy your heart may become insensible to His voice (see Prov. 29:1).

God says, " 'In a favorable time I listened to you, and in a day of salvation I have helped you.' Behold, now is the favorable time; behold, now is the day of salvation" (2 Cor. 6:2).

This is a hard word, I know. Yet it is a true word.

God's offer of grace will one day be withdrawn from those who prove unfaithful. But it will ever be open to those who faithfully respond in repentant faith and obedience.

Yes, God rejected Ephraim, but . . .

> 68 but he chose the tribe of Judah [the southern kingdom],
> Mount Zion, which he loves.
>
> 69 He built his sanctuary [the Temple, the new center of worship] like the high heavens,
> like the earth, which he has founded forever.
>
> 70 He chose David his servant
> and took him from the sheepfolds;
>
> 71 from following the nursing ewes he brought him
> to shepherd Jacob his people,
> Israel his inheritance.
>
> 72 With upright heart he shepherded them
> and guided them with his skillful hand.

That is grace extended.

While some may reject God's grace, and He may eventually withdraw His hand, still He extends His grace to those who will receive it. God goes on—ever and always—giving, for that is His nature. He always finds someone who will receive His grace by faith and demonstrate it through a life of faithful worship.

God offers you His grace in Christ. He extends to you the opportunity to be a part of what He is doing. But if you choose not to receive that grace, His plan will march onward. The only question is whether you'll be a player or not.

Always True

The strategy of Psalm 78 is not unusual in the Bible. The Hebrews often employed a review of their history to make a point. Observe the same, for example, in Psalms 105, 107 and 136.

The same pattern is also seen in the New Testament. One of the best examples is in the lengthy and legendary sermon of Stephen. When facing a hostile, unbelieving Jewish audience, Stephen employed a form that was comfortably familiar to them. In Acts 7, Stephen met their unbelief with a review of their history as a nation. Much like Psalm 78, he uses the phrase "our fathers" ten times.

His sermon is long (see Acts 7:2–53), so let me give you just his outline. Stephen told his Jewish countrymen that God gave them the Promised Land (see 7:2–36), He gave them the Law (see 7:37–43) and He gave them the Temple (see 7:44–50). Theirs had been a story of grace. God had given and given and given again. Then, like every good sermon, He moved to apply all this to the lives of his listeners. Remember, in three different ways, and using almost fifty verses of Scripture, Stephen reminded them that God had given and given and given to them.

His application? Just listen.

> You stiff-necked people, uncircumcised in heart and ears, you always resist the Holy Spirit. As your fathers did, so do you.

> Which of the prophets did your fathers not persecute? And they killed those who announced beforehand the coming of the Righteous One, whom you have now betrayed and murdered, you who received the law as delivered by angels and did not keep it. (Acts 7:51–53)

"You've been *unfaithful*! And you can't even begin to see the line of grace from which you've strayed over these generations!"

Whoa!

Their response?

"Now when they heard these things they were enraged, and they ground their teeth at him" and then "they cried out with a loud voice and stopped their ears and rushed together at him. Then they cast him out of the city and stoned him" (7:54, 57–58).

That didn't go terribly well, did it?

So, what have we learned here today?

Religious folk don't take it well when told they've misused the grace of God. They don't take it well when you show them from their own book that they've been found unfaithful to God's line of grace.

Lay it out side by side: "God gave. You ________."

Apart from divine intervention, that doesn't usually go over well.

The great question, of course, is: How will we respond? What should *we* do about these things? I suggest you take some moments alone with God and undertake the following.

First, take stock of the grace you've received from God. Make a list: "In my life, God has ________." Take your time. Make sure you include some things you might be tempted to think too obvious—like your life, health, protection, food and housing. Remember to calculate in all that He has secured and offers you in Jesus Christ.

Then, examine your response to this grace. Again, take your time. Write it down: "In the face of God's grace: I have ________." Be honest. Be thorough. How have you responded to God's grace? How far from God's line of grace have you lived your life?

Finally, take shelter in God's Shepherd.

What does that mean?

Did you notice how Asaph concluded his call to a life of faithful worship? He pointed out that not only did God choose a particular people—"the tribe of Judah" (Ps. 78:68), in a particular place—"Mount Zion, which he loves" (78:68), to make his presence manifest among them—"his sanctuary" (78:69), but additionally He selected a particular person—"He chose David" (78:70)—to guide them into this relationship. God "took him from the sheepfolds; from following the nursing ewes he brought him to shepherd Jacob his people, Israel his inheritance" (78:70–71).

Just as Asaph ended the previous psalm by referencing Moses and Aaron as God's shepherds, chosen to guide God's people into a life of worship (see Ps. 77:20), so he ends this psalm by reminding the people of their greatest earthly king, David, and his role as their shepherd.

All the way through, God has been shepherding your life, guiding you into His grace. God has done it, but He has used specific people, just as He used Moses, Aaron and David. "With upright heart [David] shepherded them and guided them with his skillful hand" (Ps. 78:72) into laying down a line of life-response that was commensurate with the grace God had extended to them. It was in this endeavor that Asaph was first recruited by David, and it was to this purpose that Asaph laid down a legacy of faithful worship that would span generations and centuries.

Of course, David, great as he was, served as a foreshadowing of God's ultimate Shepherd, the Lord Jesus Christ. He is David's ultimate son. The New Testament opens with the words "The book of the genealogy of Jesus Christ, the son of David . . ." (Matt. 1:1). Stephen recounted the grace of God to Israel saying, "So it was until the days of David" (Acts 7:45). And ultimately, as his life was ebbing away, Stephen turned to David's greater son, praying, "Lord Jesus, receive my spirit" (7:59).

Do you see what has happened? Stephen lived so close to the line of God's grace that he was only a whisper away in the end.

"And falling to his knees he cried out with a loud voice, 'Lord, do not hold this sin against them'" (7:60). "Lord," he prayed, "keep giving to these people! Keep being gracious, O Lord! Do not withdraw Your hand, for maybe this time they will respond!"

"And when he had said this, he fell asleep" (7:60).

If you haven't given yourself to Jesus in life, He won't receive you at death. All the seriousness that sweeps over you in your final moments can't replace a life lived in faithful worship to the One into whose holy presence you are about to step.

Look for the line. Get close. Get real close. Live there, faithfully. Worship Him there, forever.

Worship in Action

- Set apart some time now and undertake those exercises I just outlined.
- First, take stock of the grace you have already received from God. Annie Flint put it this way in her great hymn: "His love has no limits, His grace has no measure, His power has no boundary known unto men; For out of His infinite riches in Jesus, He giveth, and giveth, and giveth again!"[4] Take plenty of paper. Do your work well. List the evidences of God's grace in your life—the seemingly mundane and the wildly spectacular, the everyday and the life-defining, the apparently human and the obviously divine.
- Now, beside each item on that list, record your life-response to that expression of grace. What have you done about this grace? How have you responded to the stream of giving from God's throne (see Heb. 4:16).
- Finally, realize that none of us lives perfectly faithful to God. Only Jesus did that. That's why we all must run to Jesus, the Good Shepherd. He is the one who "lays down his life for the sheep" (John 10:11, 15). Where there is a disparity between grace given and your life lived faithfully in worship, seek the cleansing grace of Jesus' blood (see

1 John 1:9). Don't just slap a single sentence of confession over these things, be thorough and specific.

- Having done so, turn your heart to expressions of thanksgiving and praise to the God "who giveth, and giveth, and giveth again!"

9

Living a Life of Perplexity

Psalm 79

The game is tied—two outs in the bottom of the ninth. The opposing pitcher has filled the bases, walking your last two batters on eight straight pitches. Your man at the plate—a career .174 hitter—has worked a three-nothing count. The pitcher winds up to deliver the decisive pitch and . . . the batter swings!

At which every true baseball fan throws his hands in the air and screams, "What are you doing?"

Payday is five days away. Everybody's feeling the stretch. You stop off at a gas station on the way home from work to put a few dollars' worth in your gas tank. As you swing through the doors to pay your bill, you see your friend. He's second in line. You know he's going home to empty cupboards and a hungry family. As he reaches the register, you see him pull out his last twenty and buy . . . a lottery ticket!

You are barely able to muffle your outrage, "What are you thinking!"

Life, and how people handle it, often makes us throw our hands in the air in disbelief. How can people we love live so illogically?

But what if that someone is God? What are we to do when God is making no sense?

Remember Job? He had no clue as to why suffering befell him. Home, family, wealth, health—all of it—gone in an instant! No warning. No explanation. No inside information.

Psalm 79 was penned in perplexity.

Even a casual reader of the psalm can see that great suffering had come upon God's people, Israel. We don't know the precise date or circumstances out of which the psalm arose, but it was probably written after the armies of Nebuchadnezzar, king of Babylon, sacked Jerusalem, murdered its citizens, destroyed the city's revered structures, burned the Temple, demolished the city walls and led the survivors away to a life of exile in Babylon.

Psalm 79 shows us how to live a life of worship when all you want to do is throw your hands in the air and shout "Why?" Throughout the generations, God's people have taken up this prayer when they don't understand God's ways. There are echoes in Jeremiah's weeping prophecies.[1] It was taken up in the days of the Maccabees' great sufferings.[2]

The light of Asaph's prayer reveals a pathway leading from our perplexity to God's praise. He shows how confusion can become worship. It demonstrates how to process through three stages of perplexity and, in the end, find yourself once again before God as a worshiper.

Perplexity Interrupts Our Worship

Stage one is when perplexity interrupts our worship. It's that moment when you're so confused by God and His governance of the world that you realize you've stopped worshiping and started wondering. As you observe the details of life, it is difficult for you to discern a loving Father's hand in it all. You don't see the puzzle pieces of your life coming together into a coherent, let alone beautiful, picture. You believe that God rules in providence, but the observable evidence has, frankly, perplexed you.

Note the perplexity in the psalmist's voice as he opens the psalm.

> 1 O God, the nations have come into your inheritance;
> they have defiled your holy temple;
> they have laid Jerusalem in ruins.
>
> 2 They have given the bodies of your servants
> to the birds of the heavens for food,
> the flesh of your faithful to the beasts of the earth.
>
> 3 They have poured out their blood like water
> all around Jerusalem,
> and there was no one to bury them.
>
> 4 We have become a taunt to our neighbors,
> mocked and derided by those around us.

Take note of what perplexes the psalmist about God.

He is perplexed over *God's handling of His holy place.*

> 1 O God, the nations have come into your inheritance;
> they have defiled your holy temple;
> they have laid Jerusalem in ruins.

The land was the place of God's choosing and thus their "inheritance." The "temple" was the place of God's dwelling and thus their glory. The city of Jerusalem was the place of God's reigning and thus their security. But now "the nations" have "come into" the place that is holy to the Lord and into which He had invited His chosen people. The Babylonians "defiled" the Temple with their ungodliness. They "laid . . . in ruins" the city where God had set His name.

There were many "nations" to blame. Babylon single-handedly had carried out the atrocities, but there were many other nations all too glad to fill the stands and cheer them on. Nations like Moab, Ammon and Edom applauded the destruction of God's holy place.

For the worshiper, there is no sense to be made of this. He protests, "The land, the city, the Temple are 'Your' place, not 'ours.'"

Furthermore, the worshiper is perplexed over *God's handling of His holy people.* These ungodly invaders have, apparently with God's permission, "given the bodies of your servants to the birds of the heavens for food, the flesh of your faithful to the beasts of the earth" (Ps. 79:2).

> 3 They have poured out their blood like water
> all around Jerusalem,
> and there was no one to bury them.

The Babylonians were ruthless in conquest; wanton in the bloodshed and death of God's people. The blood of God's people ran through the streets "like run-off water" after a downpour.[3] The lifeless carcasses of the holy people of God were left as carrion. The circling shadows of vultures and buzzards framed the scene.

For the Jews, an unattended, unburied body at death was the ultimate disgrace. The scene in my mind's eye is one of those aged photos—faded and brown, tattered and worn along the edges—showing the carnage of some Civil War battlefield. Acre after acre strewn with stiffened bodies of someone's brother and another's son, laying one atop another—uncollected and unburied, frozen in their agonies by the onset of rigor mortis.

And to whom has God permitted this to be done?

To "your servants"; to "your faithful"!

No one's claiming they hadn't sinned. They had and the psalmist knew it. What he is claiming is that, "Our sin notwithstanding, we are still Your covenant people. How can You permit such things to befall us?"

And then, Asaph is further perplexed over *God's handling of His holy purpose.* God's great purpose—from eternity past through eternity future—is to demonstrate the greatness of His glory as a giver. God is love. He is a dealer in grace. But look at what has happened!

> 4 We have become a taunt to our neighbors,
> mocked and derided by those around us.

God's purpose seems to have been lost. Instead of glory redounding to God, there are three polar opposites of glory. Instead of praise, there was a "taunt" (verbal scorn, reproach, abuse). Rather than being respected, they were "mocked" (scoffing, perhaps even mimicry and derisive humor). In the place of honor, they were "derided" (the scornful belittling of something of great value as though it is worthless).

"Where in all this, O God, is Your purpose?"

When God's promises appear to be overlooked, perplexity creeps in. When His purpose seems to have been lost, the worshiper is turned aside from his adoration of God.

It's enough to make you throw your hands in the air!

Here's a suggestion. Grab a piece of blank paper. (I'm serious, do it!). Draw three dots on it. Just set the point of your pen down anywhere on the page. Point one. Now add a second dot. That's two. Add a third, making the three align in a straight line.

Now, hand the page to someone else. Ask them to add a fourth dot.

Where do you expect them to lay down the next dot?

Without consciously thinking about it, you expect it to be lined up with the other three dots. But suppose they drop it in some random corner of the page?

You don't have to have OCD for this to perplex you. With the first three dots, a pattern began to emerge. There is a silent expectation being established. You fully expect that the fourth dot will fall in line with the other three.

Then, inexplicably, it does not.

You are bewildered.

When it becomes about more than dots of ink on a blank page, when the stakes are raised, when the dots are marked with the blood of human lives laid down upon the scroll of history, suddenly the angst rises to a seemingly unbearable level.

To be honest, it's frightening. It feels a lot like doubt. There is something about it that feels almost like, dare we say it, unbelief.

But it isn't unbelief. For, despite the baffling behavior of God, we remain "your servants . . . your faithful" (Ps. 79:2). It's true; we are. Even if I can't make heads or tails out of what God is doing—or not doing. What we are in fact feeling is a necessary part of processing through a life of perplexity. It is a sometimes essential leg in the journey of life as worship.

We have to do this work and we have to do it thoroughly. If we do, it gives way ultimately to a second stage in this process.

Prayer Gives Expression to Our Perplexity

The second stage is when prayer gives expression to our perplexity. If perplexity *throws its hands* toward heaven in stunned confusion, prayer *lifts its hands* to heaven in hopeful supplication.

Observe carefully as Asaph opens his heart toward the God he does not understand. Consider the content of his prayer under four banners.

First, there are *questions*. He prays, in essence, "God, explain Yourself!"

> 5 How long, O LORD? Will you be angry forever?
> Will your jealousy burn like fire?

That's three questions to be exact (though he'll add a fourth in verse 10). Consider them seriatim. First, Asaph asks, "How long, O LORD?"

Ever asked that?

Be honest!

"How long?" is a profoundly different question than "Why?"

"How long?" doesn't imply that God is being unfair. It doesn't hint that God has been unrighteous in His dealings with His people. The question doesn't upbraid Him for an apparent lack of response to your needs.

In his more candid moments, Asaph knows they deserve what they've gotten.

He is not yet demanding that God explain Himself. Rather, his opening question simply seeks to understand the duration of the present circumstances.

The same span of time looks different when viewed from heaven than from earth. It is the opposite effect of jumping off the high dive at the swimming pool. After several hours of staring ominously upward at the high dive, you begin to self-counsel: *That isn't so high. I think I could do that.* So you make the long walk. You climb the ladder. You stand upon the dreaded plank of death. The first glance is all it takes to conclude that the same distance looks frighteningly different from above than from below!

Just the opposite is in effect when it comes to pain and the perplexity it causes. Without the perspective of heaven, the pain of earth seems interminable. Inside the pain time slows down. From inside the apparent delay, the question, "How long?" boils to the surface.

But you'll note that the question assumes God's sovereignty—that He is in control and that He knows the answer to our question. There is, even here, a hint of faith, a longing to worship.

The next question: "Will You be angry forever?"

The Bible says God is angry every day over sin (see Ps. 7:11). This isn't just Asaph's question; it's ours as well.

But be careful here.

You can't understand God's anger by measuring from earth to heaven. Human anger is tainted with selfishness and sin. God's anger is hot, but it is holy. It is not a wild, irrational, fly-off-the-handle kind of anger. It is preceded by innumerable warnings, explanations of its grounds and loving pleadings for a change of direction.

Again, there's no question about God's right to be angry. We just want to know if there will ever be a reaching of its peak and another side to our experience with Him. Just how far in the distance might the downslope of grace be?

Third question: "Will Your jealousy burn like fire?"

The Bible is clear: God is a jealous God.[4]

Don't let your mind race down the first apparent trail. Don't look at human jealousy and measure upward toward God in an attempt to understand His jealousy. Human jealousy is a perversion of God's holy jealousy.

Humanly, we are jealous of something or someone. A wife is jealous of her husband's work or of his hobby. A man may be jealous of his wife's friends.

God is jealous *over* something or *for* something. God is not jealous *of* anything, for He has no true rivals. Such jealousy would be born out of insecurity—something of which God knows nothing. No, God is jealous *over* His people.[5] His is a jealousy born of love, not insecurity. Holy jealousy is born of strength, purpose and commitment—not weakness and fear.

True, perplexity raises questions, questions which may force our hands heavenward in bewilderment. Maybe we at first threw our hands in the air in perplexity; but once there, we can keep them heavenward as we voice those questions to God in prayer.

There is a second phase to the psalmist's prayer. Let's hang the banner *vengeance* over it, for the request is "Destroy Your enemies!"

> 6 Pour out your anger on the nations
> that do not know you,
> and on the kingdoms
> that do not call upon your name!
>
> 7 For they have devoured Jacob
> and laid waste his habitation.

It is a simple request for the redirection of the anger he's just inquired about (see Ps. 79:5). The enemy "poured out" their blood like so much runoff after a deluge (see 79:3). Now Asaph prays, "Pour out Your anger on Your enemies!"

It's the same verb in both cases. "What they did with the blood of Your people, now do with Your anger upon them! They did not hold back on us, so don't You hold back on them!"

Ever felt some of that?

These people are God's enemies because they "do not know you" and "do not call upon your name" (79:6). They are idol worshipers! At least Asaph and his people—though full of pain, perplexity and questions and often failing God—worship only Him.

Now we come to our third banner—in contrast to pouring out anger on His enemies, Asaph asks God to extend grace to His people. He petitions God, "Forgive Your people!"

> 8 Do not remember against us our former iniquities;
> let your compassion come speedily to meet us,
> for we are brought very low.
>
> 9 Help us, O God of our salvation,
> for the glory of your name;
> deliver us, and atone for our sins,
> for your name's sake!

You'll note that there are two things for which Asaph seeks God's grace in forgiveness. The first is "our former iniquities" (79:8). This might refer to sins committed prior to the disaster that has befallen them. The marginal reading renders it, "the iniquities of former generations." In other words, "Lord, please don't punish us for our fathers' sins!" The second need of forgiveness is for "our sins" (79:9). They didn't need to be punished for their fathers' sins—they had enough of their own! They had taken the baton of rebellion from their fathers and run hard.

Carefully note the two ways in which Asaph asks for this forgiving grace. First he prays, "Do not remember against us" our sins (Ps. 79:8).

You've figured out by now, I hope, that there is no such thing as "forgive and forget." I know; you've heard it so often it's begun to sound like Bible. Trouble is, it's not.

God doesn't forget our sins. God knows everything. God can't "not know" something. If God forgot your sins, what if suddenly He remembered them? What? Has He misplaced them? How is it that a Being who knows everything can suddenly not know something—unless of course He knows that He doesn't know it, which would mean that He remembers what He has supposedly forgotten?

Would we be any better off in such an arrangement?

Actually the Bible's news is far better than "forgive and forget." The Scriptures teach us that God chooses not to remember our sins against us. It isn't that He doesn't know they happened, but that He simply has determined that He will never remember them against us. When He forgives you through Christ, God promises to never treat you according to your sins and failures. This good news is built upon the rock solid, everlasting commitment of the inviolable will of an infinite Being who has harnessed His power to His love, mercy and grace in covenant with you through Jesus Christ.

This kind of forgiving grace is to become the pattern of our relationships. The template has been provided: "Forgiving one another, as God in Christ forgave you" (Eph. 4:32).

At the very mention of forgiveness you may inwardly object, "I will never be able to rid from my mind the memory of ________!"

God knows that. He is not asking you to achieve the impossible. He is asking you—out of your experience of His forgiving grace—to extend to someone who has wronged you what you've already received from God. Choose not to remember their sins against them.

I have things in my past that I remember. Oh, buddy, do I remember! All too well, all too often.

Yet, by God's grace, I have forgiven. And forgiven. And forgiven. Again. And again. And God, over the passing of years, as I choose not to remember against someone what they've done to me, releases me from the grip of that pain . . . more and more . . . and more.

I'm telling you, there is real freedom from the clutches of bitterness and unforgiveness. It is real freedom! Sure, I still remember what was done to me. And sometimes—thank the Lord, less and less as the years go by—I still have to choose not to remember those offenses against those people. But God is enabling me to live in that freedom.

God is ready to extend the same grace to you.

Upon what basis can God thus forgive us (which then becomes the basis upon which we extend forgiveness to others)?

Asaph speaks to that next when he prays that God would "atone for" their sins (Ps. 79:9). The word means "to cover." That is precisely what all the sacrifices under the old covenant did—first at the Tabernacle and later in the Temple. Those sins were covered, but they were not removed. The blood of the sacrificed animal was sprinkled on the atonement seat, the cover of the ark of the covenant, which concealed the two tablets of God's law within. That law stood as the accusing standard that exposed the worshiper's failure to keep God's demands. The blood was then applied to the cover of the ark so as to symbolically come between God (whose glory was manifest above that lid) and our violence to the law of God (that lay beneath that lid). Thus, the sins of the worshipers were covered, but they were never removed.

We have a problem here, however. If, indeed, we've rightly understood the setting of this psalm, then there was no more Temple. It had been destroyed by the armies of Babylon. The Temple had been ruined, the city sacked, the people murdered or led away to exile in a foreign land. The city is in ruins. The Temple has been destroyed. They aren't even in the city and they can't go back to it, even if there was a Temple left there.

On what basis then was Asaph able to ask God to "atone for" their sins?

Asaph's prayer reminds us that, even under the Mosaic covenant, the wise knew that the blood of bulls and goats could not take away sins. Only God can do that. And thus He is called the "God of our salvation" (Ps. 79:9) or, as the NIV renders it, "God our Savior." Only "God our Savior" can take away our sins!

He prays, "Let your compassion come" (79:8). Compassion is personified as a strong warrior striding out to meet us in our sins. He assertively approaches—not to dole out judgment to us, but to extend to us love and grace and forgiveness and mercy!

God's demand for the sacrifice of those animals was a command for His worshipers to watch for the day that God our Savior would Himself stride onto the human scene—not just to cover our sins, but ultimately to remove them entirely. God accomplished this once and for all when Jesus Christ—God in human flesh—came to earth and went to the cross. He was rightly called "the Lamb of God, who *takes away* the sin of the world!" (John 1:29).

See where all this is headed? It begins with hands thrown toward heaven in dismay and perplexity. Those hands are then lifted to heaven in prayer. Some of those prayers are full of questions—questions so sharp they lance the boil of bitterness. Sometimes it isn't pretty. But the infection of the soul must be drained off.

When those prayers come full circle we begin to pray, "Lord, I want You to forgive *me*!"

Do you see it?

Let me ask you, *Where's the fourth dot going to land?*

It lands on—*glory*! He prays, "Lord, defend Your name!"

Asaph now brings to the surface a subtheme he's woven through the fabric of the psalm:

- "your name" (Ps. 79:6)
- "the glory of your name" (79:9)
- "for your name's sake" (79:9)

Increasingly, the offenders and their offenses, the sufferings of God's people and their questions all begin to fade from the worshiper's attention. They're not obliterated, but they are fainter. Incrementally, they are replaced with a different concern—the very thing that is most urgently upon God's heart. Asaph finally lets it loose in a torrent of unrest.

> 10 Why should the nations say,
> "Where is their God?"
> Let the avenging of the outpoured blood of your servants
> be known among the nations before our eyes!
>
> 11 Let the groans of the prisoners come before you;
> according to your great power, preserve those doomed to die!
>
> 12 Return sevenfold into the lap of our neighbors
> the taunts with which they have taunted you, O Lord!

"Where is their God?" That may be the most painful taunt the world can throw in our faces. It's a question of the ungodly, and a fear of the righteous, voiced often through the ages.[6] Is there an answer when God seems to be unconcerned? Unresponsive? Uninterested? What of those seasons when God seems to have forgotten His covenant mercy and promises?

We're not alone when we pray, "God, defend Your name!"

In view of this struggle, I want to consider the long journey the psalmist has made from his opening cries to this crescendo of concern. He's moved from utter dismay and perplexity to laying hold of the one thing which is most precious to God. He began with calls for vengeance toward others and moved into pleadings of forgiveness for himself. He's opened with questions which he demanded God answer and has now come to God's own glory which he calls on Him to defend.

Do you see the *journey*?

Sometimes we view prayer as a product—we can't pull it out until the product is perfectly honed and refined. So, because what's on the inside is messy, we choose not to pray.

Here's my counsel: Ditch the prayer-as-a-product idea. Prayer is a process.

We too often look at prayer as if it is a portrait—perfectly timed, primped, retouched. View prayer rather as a travelogue. Prayer doesn't capture the picture of us at our pious-best. Prayer is the journey that gets us from the painful present to the presence of God.

See this picture? This is where I first opened my heart up to God. Yeah, I know. I was a mess. But look at this one, or maybe this one. Here is where I started to turn a corner with God. And here—would you look at that! What? Oh, yes, I know. I'm glad you noticed—the early pictures are full of me and the latter ones are almost always of God.

I challenge you to view prayer not just as an outcome, but as a process; not just as a destination, but as a journey. And what a journey it is! Hands once thrown upward in perplexity are now lifted in prayer. Those prayers aren't always neat and tidy, but they transport us from questioning God to defending His name, from fixation on our pain to passion for God's glory. Behold the power of worship as a healing, sanctifying process.

That is not to say that worship is remedial. Worship as therapy? God forbid! That would prostitute worship into a man-centered abomination. What I am saying is that when God is returned to His rightful place at the center of everything and I actively become wrapped up in extolling Him as such, He brings me from where neither one of us wants me to be to the place I was designed and created for. God first. God always. God in everything. God over all. God all-glorious.

When we return to reverence, we begin to see reality as it is in actuality. Reverence defines reality, never the other way around. And there is no wholeness apart from reality. When God is lifted up, He pours out His healing grace.

Yet even this is not the end of the process. Perplexity becomes prayer. Prayer processes through to an ever-increasing focus Godward and this can only end in praise.

Praise Returns Us to Our Purpose

When the journey deposits us back in the place of worship, we find ourselves home. Praise returns us to our purpose. This is the third stage.

> 13 But we your people, the sheep of your pasture,
> will give thanks to you forever;
> from generation to generation we will
> recount your praise.

What began with "groans" (Ps. 79:11) over all the perplexities of life (see 79:1–4) became the prayer that opened with questions but ended in a defense of God's glory (see 79:5–12). Such prayer always lands us in the place of "thanks" and "praise" (79:13).

Asaph delighted in two great gifts of God. The first, *God chose us*—"we are your people"! Despite my circumstances, I am still His! The second, *God cares for us*— "the sheep of your pasture"! Despite my circumstances, I am still under His care!

For these simple, but life-altering graces we "will give thanks to you forever." Indeed, "from generation to generation we will recount your praise" (79:13).

Dr. Ravi Zacharias, the renowned apologist, tells of an experience from his childhood which has lived on in his conscience for many decades. Ravi knew little to nothing of the Christian faith as a child, but was asked to play the part of Joseph at the nativity play that Christmas. Responsibly, he arrived early at the church. There was time to burn, so he decided to take a look around the cathedral.

While taking in the beauty of the place, Ravi spotted a bowl of biscuits sitting on the altar table. He grabbed up a handful of the wafers and began munching on them as he gazed at the awe-inspiring structure that engulfed him. About that time the priest appeared. Young Ravi greeted him—crumbs on his face giving him away.

The priest stopped Ravi and angrily shouted, "What are you doing?"

Ravi, as shocked by the priest's eruption as he was of Ravi's "snack," exclaimed, "I'm Joseph in the nativity play!" Apparently this wasn't what the priest was after. So he interrogated him further, "What are those?" By now Ravi was mortified. He recalls, "He led me to the vestry in the back of the church, where he let me have it. It was one of the worst tongue-lashings I had ever experienced. Yet, I still had no idea what I had done wrong. He kept using the word 'sacrilege' again and again, but I didn't know what it meant. The torrent of words was so vehement I was convinced he was going to call the police."

Years later, having become a Christian, Ravi read a definition of sacrilege (still able to hear the echo of the priest's words in his heart). The writer, says Ravi, assigned the word a twofold meaning. First, sacrilege refers to taking something that belongs to God and using it profanely. This is what the priest believed he'd happened upon that December day in the cathedral. But the second meaning portrays sacrilege in its worst form: taking something and giving it to God when it means absolutely nothing to you.[7]

My friend, hear me clearly. The pains of life, and the perplexities they give birth to, are not mistakes. They are not details overlooked by a harried God, too busy to do anything about them. The pains of life are God's means of seasoning and maturing our worship. The pains and perplexities of your life enable your worship to mean something to you.

It is a relatively simple thing to praise God in the sunshine. Thus, sometimes God sends dark clouds over our lives.

Why?

All the reasons are beyond our ability to know, but one reason is that God is raising the value—both to Him and to us—of the praise we offer to Him. The perplexities of life add value to our worship. The dark clouds are not a sign that God does not love you, but that He does! The trials, pain and perplexities of life are not God crossing out His price tag on your value, but His way of raising the price tag on the love you express to Him through your worship.

Pain saves us from sacrilege. Pain is the antidote to empty, meaningless, valueless worship.

There are three ways you can lift your hands to heaven. You can throw them up in perplexity—and sometimes you can't help but do so. You can lift them in prayer—and this is how God rescues us from the cul-de-sac of perplexity. You can raise your hands in praise—and this is how God leads you home to Himself.

Worship in Action

- Begin at the beginning. Make a list of what bothers you about how God is dealing with things in your life.
- Express to God what you *feel* about those things. Not how you think you should feel about them, but how you actually feel about them. Be honest. Be authentic.
- Tell God why you think you feel that way about these things. Make your case. Tell God why you think it makes sense to feel this way about these matters.
- Take your time here. Take an hour. Take a week! Take as long as you need.
- As you do, move with God from your questions and feelings to your sins. Ask God to show them to you. How have you contributed to the issues?

Own what He shows you. Receive the grace of His forgiveness through Christ.

- As you receive God's grace afresh, extend it to the others in your life. Remember, this is a decision, not a feeling. Remember, you may not forget, but you can—by God's grace—decide not to remember the offense against that person. Settle it with God. Nail it down.
- Now talk with God about how all of this—their sin and yours, your pain and that of others—reflects upon God's reputation in the world. Pray through until you know you care more about God's glory than your feelings.
- Rejoice that your circumstances—however painful they may be—have not severed you from Jesus Christ. They have not canceled out His care for you and His control of your life. Taking up Romans 8:31–39, praise Him for this faithfulness.

10

Living a Life of Revival

Psalm 80

Excitedly, the five of us jumped in our loaded van and headed south. Vacation! In short order, the euphoria gave way to slumber for everyone else and I found myself alone in a van full of sleeping travelers. No problem—the solitude and the scenery were a balm.

As we passed over the river and out of Ohio, the scenic vistas of West Virginia broke forth around me. Deep, cleansing breaths filled my lungs as mountain peaks, thick forests and bubbling streams filled my vision. Quietly I hummed, "Almost heaven, West Virginia . . ."

At one point, I took note of a lovely little church nestled into a mountainside along the right side of the road. *Hmm, what a quaint little building.*

But it wasn't far into the Mountain State that I needed to visit the boys' room, so I found an off-ramp and pulled into a rest area. Everyone awakened from their naps, slid on their shoes, did their business and quickly resumed their slumbering positions as I pulled the rig back onto the interstate.

Zzzzzzzzzz . . .

Drinking in the mountain view, I forged ahead, the captain of this wagon train! I resumed the posture of the awestruck wonderer—mountain peaks, wooded valleys, gurgling streams, nature's beauty encircling us.

Then I noted another lovely little church—on the left side of the interstate.

Hmm, what a quaint little church building.

You know, that looks a great deal like the church I saw a ways back, only on my right.

Wait! What?

Sure enough. Lost in wonder, love and praise for all-things-vacation, I had unthinkingly reentered the interstate going the wrong direction. We were headed back north—toward Ohio and home!

It wasn't *similar* to the church I'd seen earlier. It *was* the church I had seen earlier! Unfortunately, Julie felt the vehicle slowing and, as I turned off on the next exit ramp, she asked through bleary eyes, "What's up?"

Indeed!

Unable to concoct a convincing story on the spur of the moment, I went with the truth. I fessed up. She was in vacation mode and just laughed it off. Best of all, we agreed not to tell the kids we'd just wasted an hour of their life.

Now here's my question for you: Is it possible we're headed the wrong direction and don't know it?

By "we" I mean us—God's people, Christ-followers.

It's a rather unsettling question. It would rather change the whole ride wouldn't it?

Is it even possible?

It certainly happened with God's people Israel. We're told so in Psalm 80.

But that isn't really breaking news. The entire Bible echoes this story. Moses warned of this possibility. The prophets confronted a wandering nation with this admonition. Yet they happily went their way.

The wrong way? Nah! Couldn't be!

Need I mention that all the while they were going through the motions of worship? They retained all the forms of worship. They had the Temple, offered sacrifices, observed the feasts, prayed the prayers and recited the Scriptures. Yet they were not living a life of worship.

That is our stated objective—living life as worship. Not just going to worship, but living a life of worship. Not just saying prayers, but entering God's presence. Not just singing songs, but God inhabiting our praises.

Arriving at a life of worship may require admitting we're headed the wrong direction.

Pictures of Our Journey in the Wrong Direction

Join me as we join Asaph. He's pulled out the picture album and wants us to see a few photos of our journey in the wrong direction. Let me warn you, however. These are not photos from the family vacation at the beach. They are more like crash-site images broadcast on the evening news—pictures from a head-on collision with someone headed the wrong way down the interstate.

> 1 Give ear, O Shepherd of Israel,
> you who lead Joseph like a flock.
> You who are enthroned upon the cherubim, shine forth.
>
> 2 Before Ephraim and Benjamin and Manasseh,
> stir up your might
> and come to save us!
>
> 4 O Lord, God of hosts,
> how long will you be angry with your people's prayers?

5 You have fed them with the bread of tears
and given them tears to drink in full measure.

6 You make us an object of contention for our neighbors,
and our enemies laugh among themselves.

What is this first picture?

It is the image of *an aimless flock with an angry Shepherd.* Israel is the flock, God the Shepherd. Israel had once been a beloved flock with a glad Shepherd, but no longer.

The Lord is still their Shepherd. God has not changed. But clearly something has changed. God is now angry with His flock. What specifically is He angry over?

His "people's prayers."

Israel had the forms of worship (prayers), but something was amiss. The forms, through which they once offered worship and received grace, now made God angry and drew His discipline (see Ps. 80:5–6).

Disconcerting, isn't it?

But there is another picture here. See if you can identify it.

8 You brought a vine out of Egypt;
you drove out the nations and planted it.

9 You cleared the ground for it;
it took deep root and filled the land.

10 The mountains were covered with its shade,
the mighty cedars with its branches.

11 It sent out its branches to the sea
and its shoots to the River.

12 Why then have you broken down its walls,
so that all who pass along the way pluck its fruit?

13 The boar from the forest ravages it,
and all that move in the field feed on it.

14 Turn again, O God of hosts!
  Look down from heaven, and see;
have regard for this vine,
15 the stock that your right hand planted,
  and for the son whom you made strong for yourself.

Here we have the picture of *an untended vine with a disengaged Gardener.*

Israel had once been a beautiful vine with a doting Gardener. It was stock imagery for the prophets of Israel.[1]

Look closely at Asaph's image and you'll observe the lifecycle of the vine. There is their past—with Egypt, the Exodus, the Promised Land and the establishment of the kingdom of David and Solomon (see Ps. 80:8–11). There is Israel's present—a vine with walls broken down, left vulnerable to any predator who passes their way (see 80:12–15). The picture is of a wild boar rooting and ravaging the vine. A boar, under Mosaic law, was unclean and may well represent the great Gentile power of their age, Assyria. Then you can clearly see Israel's future (see 80:16–18), which we'll look into momentarily.

These were sad, though accurate, pictures of the nation of Israel.

Some profound questions linger as we close the photo album. Is there any resemblance to your local church in these pictures? You are not disowned by God, but does He seem distant? Where are the offspring of the sheep? Where the fruit of the vine? Where is the life one should experience in worship of God? What is your trajectory as a local fellowship?

Thankfully, "The Lord disciplines the one he loves" (Heb. 12:6). That is good news. Still, there is no denying it—the pictures are grim.

Recently, we went through another of those sad stories that too often seem to fill the headlines: *Woman missing, feared abducted by her boyfriend.* The authorities emblazoned his likeness across every available media.

This time, when I looked at his picture, I said, "This guy is toast. His eyes are too unique!"

Sure enough. Within a week he'd been taken into custody. He'd fled, grown a thick, dark beard and radically changed his appearance. But there was no mistaking the eyes!

The eyes always give us away.

Is there anything about looking at these pictures that's like looking in a mirror? Do your eyes betray you?

Problems of Our Journey in the Wrong Direction

Embedded in the background of these pictures and woven throughout the psalm we have a repeated refrain.

A refrain?

Sure! If you can still get your hands on a hymn book these days, turn randomly through its pages. You'll repeatedly find hymns with a refrain that follows the verses. The word refrain comes from an old French word meaning to "break off" or "repeat."[2] Musically, a refrain periodically breaks off the song and repeats something.

Three times Asaph breaks off his prayer and repeats himself.

"Restore us, O God; let your face shine, that we may be saved!" (Ps. 80:3).

"Restore us, O God of hosts; let your face shine, that we may be saved!" (Ps. 80:7).

"Restore us, O LORD God of hosts! Let your face shine, that we may be saved!" (80:19).

Three times the same prayer is offered. Each time Asaph confesses three things.

First, Asaph admits, *We're going the wrong direction.*

The prayer?

Three times: "Restore us."

The need?

Repentance!

This is the twelfth most often used verb in the entire Old Testament.[3] One scholar says, "better than any other verb it combines in itself the two requisites of repentance: to turn from evil and to turn to the good."[4] It can speak either of turning from God and toward sin or, conversely, of turning from evil and to God.

But there's more here. The form of the verb in Hebrew is causative. The point, then, is that we cannot turn ourselves back to God; He must turn us back. We must pray that God might cause us to be turned back to Him. Our inability does not cancel out our responsibility, but reminds us that we do not have the ability to do what we most desperately need as fallen people. We must turn back to God, but that begins with admitting to Him (and ourselves) that we can't do so if left to ourselves. Repentance begins not with power, but powerlessness; not with our ability, but our inability. Repentance begins with the admission that I can't even repent without God's grace! This is why the Bible presents repentance as a gift that God grants.[5]

Our need is repentance, not self-reformation.

It is as if we are barreling the wrong way down the Interstate and we can't find an off-ramp. We'll surely die if we continue the direction we're going, but we just can't manage to turn around!

So at least stop and pray! Cry out, "God, I am headed the wrong way and I don't even possess the ability to turn myself around!"

Second, Asaph prays, *We're standing in the wrong place.*

The prayer?

Three times: "Let your face shine."

The need?

Grace!

Asaph echoes the famous blessing pronounced by Aaron (and the priests that followed him) over God's people:

> The LORD bless you and keep you;
> the LORD make his face to shine upon you
> and be gracious to you;
> the LORD lift up his countenance upon you
> and give you peace.
>
> (Num. 6:24–26)

When praying "let your face shine," we are asking God to smile upon us again, to let us live under His favor once again, to allow us to stand chest deep in the flow of that river of mercy and grace that comes down from His throne upon those He loves.

How is that going to happen?

We have to move ourselves to the place where that river flows. We must reposition ourselves to where those showers fall.

Jesus told us that the Father "sends rain on the just and on the unjust" (Matt. 5:45; see Acts 14:17). In His general grace, God lets something of His goodness be tasted by all His creatures (even those in rebellion).

But God has declared that His special, saving, covenant grace will fall only in one place. If you want in on that grace, you have to move to that singular location where He has made that rain fall, that river flow. To borrow a line from *My Fair Lady,* "The rain in Spain stays mainly in the plain!" So if you want to get wet in Spain, your best bet is not going to be a trip to the mountains.[6] Where has God said His personal, special, covenant grace will fall? Within the circle of repentance. And nowhere else.

The problem is not only that we're headed in the wrong direction, but also that we're standing in the wrong place. For that reason, Asaph says, thirdly, *We're headed toward the wrong outcome.*

The prayer?

Three times: "That we may be saved."

The need?

In a word: Deliverance!

Okay, but "saved" from what?

When we see the word "saved" in the Bible we tend to think of individual spiritual salvation. While we must always personally apply God's saving work in our own lives, the verb is used throughout the Bible in a number of ways. In this case it probably had more to do with deliverance from the calamity that was hurtling toward them as a nation—conquest by the Gentile powers of Assyria and Babylon, the destruction of their Temple and exile to their pagan lands.

In what sense, then, may we make Asaph's prayer our own? What is it that we need to be "saved" from? We too need to be saved from the crash at the end of our current, spiritual trajectory. We need to be delivered from the head-on collision with reality that is rushing toward us in our flight from God and our pursuit of a life independent of Him. We need to be saved from the sad fate that befalls most churches over time—self-centeredness and the resulting discipline of the Lord.

These three things are true. We're headed in the wrong direction, standing in the wrong place and headed toward the wrong outcome.

And we can't do anything about it!

We're not going to work our way out of this mess. We're not going to plan our way out, seminar our way out, think our way out, vision-cast our way out, give our way out, dream our way out or strategically plan our way out.

Asaph is clear—*only God can help us now.*

He might use some of those tools along the way, but only He can save us from what we've gotten ourselves into.

Please note carefully, these are *we*-things, not just *me*-things. This speaks to us not just as individuals, but to us collectively as God's people.

The good folks at Life Action Ministries recently issued "A Declaration of National Spiritual Emergency." I've signed my name to verify that I believe they are correct. Here is a portion of their declaration.

> With heavy hearts, we recognize that the church in America is in a state of spiritual emergency. Like the churches warned in Revelation, we have become lukewarm and compromised, and the light of our witness has grown dim.
>
> We confess that despite access to more resources and biblical teaching than any other group of believers in history, we are not characterized by the supernatural power of the Holy Spirit. And we acknowledge our lack of widespread impact for Christ on our lost and disintegrating culture.
>
> But God is waking us from our slumber and mobilizing us to pray earnestly for revival. Together, we desire to travel the narrow road of brokenness, humility, and repentance.
>
> In desperation for God, we cry out for the extraordinary work of the Holy Spirit in our day. We believe that true revival is the only hope to reverse our spiritual recession and enable us once again to display the beauty of Jesus Christ and His gospel throughout the world.

Because we believe that only Christ can save, heal, and revive, we pledge to:

- TURN—in humble repentance from every sin God reveals to us
- PRAY—with urgency for spiritual recovery and awakening
- UNITE—with other believers in spreading the hope of Christ-centered revival.[7]

The declaration ends with this prayer: "Lord, send revival, and let it begin in us!"

We must come to the awareness of and admission that, only God can change our direction, alter our standing and give us a new future.

God can and will do so, as we repent. Just how does He intend to do so?

Prescriptions for Our Journey in the Wrong Direction

In the closing verses of the psalm, Asaph hints at the prescription God writes for us. They are just that, hints—clues that point to what is revealed in fuller detail elsewhere in the Bible, a sketch which is drawn more completely later in Scripture. Asaph's outline is filled in and completed by later writers of God's Word.

> 14 Turn again, O God of hosts!
> Look down from heaven, and see;
> have regard for this vine,
> 15 the stock that your right hand planted,
> and for the son whom you made strong for yourself.
>
> 16 They have burned it with fire; they have cut it down;
> may they perish at the rebuke of your face!

> 17 But let your hand be on the man of your right hand,
> the son of man whom you have made strong for yourself!
>
> 18 Then we shall not turn back from you;
> give us life, and we will call upon your name!

When Asaph calls upon God to look upon "this vine" (Ps. 80:14), he is clearly referring to Israel. But notice that in a moment the "vine" (80:14) becomes "the son" (80:15) who becomes "the man" (80:17) and who eventually is designated "the son of man" (80:17).

Did you catch that?

- "this vine" becomes . . .
- "the son" which becomes . . .
- "the man" which becomes . . .
- "the son of man"

These terms could refer to the nation of Israel and at times did, but they are also terms that increasingly came to refer to an individual. The development of these terms is much like the designation "servant" in Isaiah chapters 41–53. In Isaiah 41, the reference is clearly to the nation of Israel as a whole, but by chapter 53 Isaiah is plainly speaking not of Israel as a nation, but of a special, God-sent, Spirit-anointed individual who would suffer and die, making atonement for His people's sins, thus reconciling them to God.

The whole of the Bible reveals that person's name—Jesus Christ!

So too here in Psalm 80. These loaded terms refer to the nation, but are ultimately only fulfilled in the person of the Messiah, Jesus of Nazareth. Thus, in the person of Jesus, God has provided all we will ever need to be delivered out of ourselves and the mess we've created and into God's grace-laden purpose for our lives.

In Jesus, *God provided someone to become what we've never been able to be.*

Take the "vine" imagery. Clearly it refers to Israel in verses 8–14. This is, as I've pointed out, true in many other places in the Hebrew Bible. Yet by the New Testament Jesus rightly could declare, "I am the vine" (John 15:5). What Israel never could be, Jesus had become—in her place, on her behalf, as her Savior. What we—and I'm including us Gentiles as well—were created to be, we have forfeited by sin. We cannot recapture that in our own power or by our own efforts, no matter how sincere. God, however, gave His Son to become what we've never been able to be. When we turn from our self-governing, independent ways and entrust ourselves to Jesus as God's provision for our salvation, God places us "in Christ" so that His merits and righteousness are counted to be ours as we are found by faith "in Him."

In Jesus, *God provided someone in a place we've never been able to attain.*

Asaph speaks of "the man of your right hand" (Ps. 80: 17). The right hand was the place of favor, authority and power. The New Testament tells us we have such a one in the Lord Jesus. We read that "after making purification for sins, he sat down at the right hand of the Majesty on high" (Heb. 1:3). God "raised us up with him and seated us with him in the heavenly places in Christ Jesus" (Eph. 2:6). "Christ Jesus is the one who died—more than that, who was raised—who is at the right hand of God, who indeed is interceding for us" (Rom. 8:34). Jesus "is able to save to the uttermost those who draw near to God through him, since he always lives to make intercession for them" (Heb. 7:25).

In Jesus, *God provided someone to do what we could never do.*

Asaph speaks of "the son of man whom you have made strong for yourself" (Ps. 80:17). In union with Christ, we have all the grace, wisdom, strength and hope we will ever need. Because of God's grace in Christ, "I can do all things through him who strengthens me" (Phil. 4:13). Strength is not just something Jesus gives, but something He is within us. Righteousness is not just something Jesus gives, but something He is for us and within us. Holiness is not just something Jesus possesses, but something He makes true of us as He dwells within us (see 1 Cor. 1:30).

What is it we need?

We need God to "give us life" (Ps. 80:18). Or, as a number of other English translations render it, we need God to "revive us."[8]

Our word *revive* derives from Latin. The compound word is made up of the prefix *re-* (again) and the word *vivere* (to live).[9]

We need God to give us life again. The life we once knew with Him—the life that we forfeited through our independent, self-directing, sinful ways. We need the life that is Jesus.

And when God revives us what will happen?

Asaph's simplicity is powerful: "We will call upon your name" (Ps. 80:18). If I may rephrase—we will worship God.

Do you see? *Living a life of worship requires living a life of returning to God.* Again and again we must return to the place of utter dependence upon Jesus, the One who indwells us by His Spirit, who alone gives us life, who alone enables us to attain life as worship.

Worship in Action

- Take some time right now to bow yourself before God. Represent your heart attitude in your physical posture, if you are able. Put your knees on the floor, your face to the ground.
- Turn to God through Christ and confess your need. Having thoroughly done so, confess also the great need of the collective body of believers that is your local church.
- Just what turning again to God means is unique to each individual or congregation. Ask God to make that clear to you for your own life. Ask Him also to make it plain to your church leaders and fellow members for your gathered identity as God's people.
- Ask God to show you how you can give physical, verbal or other outward expression to your inward turning to God. Remember, you are turning *from something* and you are turning *to someone.* Ask God to reveal to you how you can make this obvious.
- Stay before God until you know that when you do rise you won't be found in the same place spiritually as when you went low before God.

11

Living a Life of Listening

Psalm 81

Next Sunday, join in the worship at your local church. Or, if you don't have a church you regularly attend, find one to visit.

Then—right there in the middle of it all, as the worship is unfolding—ask yourself a simple question: *Why do we do this?*

I'm serious.

I've been leading people in worship for over thirty years. So you might think it odd that I invite you to ask such a question. Yet we need this, for there may be something worse than not worshiping God. That would be worshiping God thoughtlessly, meaninglessly—taking up God's name in vain even while we "worship."

It's a legitimate question: *Why do we do it?*

Or more to the point, why does God *call* us to worship Him? No, it's more than even that—why does God *command* us to worship Him?

C.S. Lewis confessed that before he became a believer and even for a while after, he was a bit put off, embarrassed even, by the insistent call of God in the psalms for us to praise Him. It seemed, he said, a bit like a vain person fishing for compliments. In time, however, he came to realize that praising God is only doing rightly the very thing we already love to do in almost every other realm of life.[1]

When you enjoy a great meal at a good restaurant, you tell others about it. You rave about the salmon or the steak. You gush about the ambiance. You commend the service. You may even write an online review so others will take pleasure in what you've enjoyed.

Your vacation turns out fantastic. A faraway look fills your eyes upon your return. You race to post your pictures online. You relive the vacation in the praises you pass on about the beauty you've seen, the rest you've gained and the fun you've enjoyed.

You find some joint that serves outstanding frozen yogurt. You can't keep the secret! "Have you ever been to Bob's Frozen Yogurt?" "No? Oh, you've got to go!" "The flavor of the day last Thursday was double-chocolate-pecan-marshmallow-caramel-fudge-delight!"

There is something about sharing the experience, retelling it, praising what you've enjoyed that not only allows you to relive the pleasure, but that actually brings it to a crescendo. *Apart from praise, pleasure is muted.*

C.S. Lewis realized that we humans were made to enjoy—that is to say, praise—everything (see 1 Tim. 6:17).[2] That goes supremely, of course, for God Himself, the Creator of all else. He is the all-satisfying One; the only truly satisfying One. Thus, praising God is not just expressing delight, but is actually the culmination and zenith of all delight.

Take, for example, the vacationing pastor, who, while away, enjoyed playing several rounds of golf. In fact, away from the watchful eyes of the congregation and his denominational leaders, he decided to live on the wild side for once—and went golfing on a Sunday morning! Toward the end of his round, he stroked his first ever hole in one. He danced a jig, pumped his arms and generally acted the fool. It was wonderful! Then, just as he was fishing his ball from the cup, it struck him—and sucked all the joy out of his feat—he could never tell anyone back home what he'd accomplished.

Psalm 81 begins with a call to worship, the very thing that made C.S. Lewis uncomfortable in the early days of his faith. Our worship services also often begin with a summons for God's people to give Him the worship that is due Him. Hear God, then, in this opening call to worship.

> 1 Sing aloud to God our strength;
> shout for joy to the God of Jacob!
>
> 2 Raise a song; sound the tambourine,
> the sweet lyre with the harp.
>
> 3 Blow the trumpet at the new moon,
> at the full moon, on our feast day.
>
> 4 For it is a statute for Israel,
> a rule of the God of Jacob.
>
> 5 He made it a decree in Joseph
> when he went out over the land of Egypt.

Come and Worship!

God does here what He does throughout Scripture—calls us to worship Him. Though this is an ancient call to worship, it has contemporary application to us as the people of God. Note that God calls us to come and worship with *regularity*.

It might not immediately be obvious to our twenty-first-century and largely Gentile eyes, but this psalm was probably written for and was regularly used in the set pattern of Jewish worship. The Jews had three great annual feasts which they celebrated in worship to the Lord. This particular psalm was a call to worship for use on one of those "feast day[s]" (80:3).

There is some debate as to which of the three feasts it was used for, but most agree it was used as a call to worship at the time of the Feast of Trumpets or Tabernacles which occurred annually in the fall of the year, around September and October.

On the first day of the month (the new moon), known as Rosh Hashanah, "the trumpet" sounded (80:3). This constituted the first day of the Jewish civil New Year. On the tenth of the month, Yom Kippur, the Day of Atonement was observed. It was Israel's most solemn day of the year. From the fifteenth—the time of "the full moon" (80:3) until the twenty-second day, they commemorated the Feast of Tabernacles. It was a joyful harvest celebration associated with the wilderness wanderings. It was to remind the Jews of God's care and provision in their journey through the wilderness.

All very interesting. But so what?

Fair enough. I share this to point out that worship, then and now, is intended to be entered into with regularity. Worship is not merely a matter of emotions felt, but arises out of blessings received. Worship is not a glandular condition, but a response to grace extended. God perpetually pours out His mercies to us, so we ought to perpetually, regularly worship Him.

God also calls us to come and worship *with diversity*.

Knowing this background for the psalm helps us understand what is involved in God's solicitation of worship. When reading the opening verses of the psalm, it may sound highly repetitive to us, as if the lines repeat the same idea over and over. In actuality it may be saying something quite distinct to the different people who were each to play unique roles in the worship.

First there was a call to *the people* generally—"Sing aloud to God our strength; shout for joy to the God of Jacob!" (Ps. 81:1).

Then came the call to *the Levites* as the official singers and instrumentalists—"Raise a song; sound the tambourine, the sweet lyre with the harp" (81:2).

Finally there came God's call to *the priests*—"Blow the trumpet at the new moon, at the full moon, on our feast day" (81:3). It was the business of the priests to take up the shofar and sound the start of the celebration "at the new moon" and to call the people to begin the Feast of Tabernacles "at the full moon."[3]

Okay, great! But again—so what?

We may not be Jewish, a Levite or an old covenant priest, but we can deduce the principle—we don't all play the same part in worship, but we all do have a part to play.

Picture something similar in our context: a series of calls to worship might first be directed to the entire gathered people of God, then a call is spoken out to the worship team/band ("Hey media techs, get the sound turned up!") and then finally a call is issued to the ushers, Sunday school teachers, elders, Scripture readers, prayers, givers, etc. Everyone—each with his own contribution to make—hears the call: "It is time to worship our God!"

Some sing, others shout, someone rattles a tambourine, another strums a lyre or plucks a harp. Yet others send their breath through wind instruments and a number clap their hands—but everyone has something to offer in worship. Unless each one is awakened to contribute his or her part, our corporate worship is muted.

We can, then, deduce also that God calls us to come and worship *with individuality.*

If you don't do your part, our worship is muted and stunted. Each one was called and involved. It takes each one in the congregation, everyone in the worship team/band, all the technicians, the pastors, all the people who invite others to join them. Our praise is corporate, but the responsibility is individual.

God calls us also to come and worship *under authority.*

There are several verbs here that are stated as commands: "Sing" and "shout" (Ps. 81:1), "raise a song" and "sound" (81:2) and "blow" (81:3). What is more, these are called "a statute," "a rule" and a "decree" (81:4, 5) from God—terms normally used to describe God's law.

The call to worship is an invitation, but it's not merely an invitation. This is not a suggestion. The call to worship is a command! To fail to heed the call is to disobey God!

Then too God calls us to come and worship *with audibility.*

You'll notice that this isn't something that can be fulfilled privately, quietly and personally. Thus by "audibility" I mean our worship becomes something that can be heard.

Such worship makes a racket!

It is to be offered "aloud" with a "shout" (81:1). We are to "raise a song" and "blow the trumpet" (81:2, 3).

There is a place in worship for quietness and stillness, but it is a place. Quiet stillness is fully legitimate and regularly appropriate in worship, but it does not occupy the whole space or even the primary place in corporate worship. To stand in the congregation of God's worshiping people and not at least make *some* joyful noise is to flout God.

God also calls us to come and worship *in community*.

Jews were required to travel to Jerusalem to worship at their God-given annual feasts. Both the journey to and experience in Jerusalem became an experience of community.

Remember when Jesus was just a boy and, after the feast, His family started toward home with the other pilgrims, but Jesus stayed on in Jerusalem (see Luke 2:41–51). He was separated from His parents and they didn't even realize it for two days! It is hard, in our modern culture of danger and distrust to picture responsible parents allowing that to happen. So it only reinforces what an experience in community all this was.

The Bible commands us to private worship. But private worship alone does not fulfill Scripture's call.

We've all been rebuffed when inviting someone to join us at church: "I can worship God at home (in nature, on the golf course or wherever else they'd rather be) as well as I can in a church!"

I'll be the first to say that whenever you are at home, in nature or on the golf course (or anywhere else for that matter), your heart ought to be going out to the Lord in worship. But it is silliness to think that this fulfills God's call to worship.

Nowhere does the New Testament permit me to hive myself off with only the people I like, the songs I prefer, performed in the styles I favor (and in so doing keep away from those that I don't appreciate) and still legitimately call it worship. Such an arrangement turns the body of Christ away from the Savior as the center of their attention and sets their focus instead upon my preferences. It demands that they mold their "worship" to my likes. True, worship may be taking place—but it may be offered to the creature, rather than the Creator.

The Bible still says, "Let us consider how to stir up one another to love and good works, not neglecting to meet together, as is the habit of some, but encouraging one another, and all the more as you see the Day drawing near" (Heb. 10:24–25).

Then too God calls us to come and worship *in responsibility*.

Our English word *response* comes from a Latin word meaning "answer."[4] Our worship is an "answer" or "response" to something.

Why were the Jews to worship God? Why are *we*?

For them, it all sprang from when God "went out over the land of Egypt" (Ps. 81:5). It was then that God "redeemed" His people Israel out of slavery. It was a sheer act of grace.

That act of redemption is a picture of the broader, more foundational redemption God achieved through His Son Jesus Christ on the cross. Worship is our response of gratitude for God's redeeming grace.

Worship disconnected from grace is religion. Worship launched from the springboard of grace is reverent relationship.

Come and Listen!

God calls us to come and worship Him. True, but actually God sets before us two appeals. One is to come and worship; the other to come and listen. God calls us to hear and heed Him.

> 5 I hear a language I had not known:
>
> 6 "I relieved your shoulder of the burden;
> your hands were freed from the basket.
>
> 7 In distress you called, and I delivered you;
> I answered you in the secret place of thunder;
> I tested you at the waters of Meribah. *Selah*
>
> 8 Hear, O my people, while I admonish you!
> O Israel, if you would but listen to me!

9 There shall be no strange god among you;
you shall not bow down to a foreign god.

10 I am the Lord your God,
who brought you up out of the land of Egypt.
Open your mouth wide, and I will fill it.

11 But my people did not listen to my voice;
Israel would not submit to me.

12 So I gave them over to their stubborn hearts,
to follow their own counsels.

13 Oh, that my people would listen to me,
that Israel would walk in my ways!

14 I would soon subdue their enemies
and turn my hand against their foes.

15 Those who hate the Lord would cringe toward him,
and their fate would last forever.

16 But he would feed you with the finest of the wheat,
and with honey from the rock I would satisfy you."

The translators have placed quotation marks beginning in verse 6. This signals that someone's—in this case God's—actual words are being cited. So look at what is enclosed by those quotation marks! Do you *see* the words about *hearing*? *Observe* the words about *listening*? They are scattered throughout Asaph's prayer:

- "I hear" (Ps. 81:5).
- "Hear, O my people" (81:8).
- "Listen to me" (81:8).
- "My people did not listen to my voice" (81:11).
- "Listen to me" (81:13).

This informs us that *listening is a test to pass.*

God speaks of His actions in delivering Israel from Egypt:

> 6 I relieved your shoulder of the burden;
> your hands were freed from the basket.
>
> 7 In distress you called, and I delivered you.

He then says, "I answered you in the secret place of thunder" (Ps. 81:7). Of what is He speaking?

This is probably a reference to His speaking on Mount Sinai when He gave the law to Moses (see Exod. 19:16–19; 20:18).

Asaph then quotes God as saying, "*I tested you* at the waters of Meribah" (Ps. 81:7). God had spoken at Sinai. Then He led them into the wilderness to bring them eventually to the Promised Land. Twice along the way—once at the beginning and once forty years later at the end of their wilderness wanderings—the people questioned God and His appointed spokesmen (see Exod. 17:1–7; Num. 20:1–13). In doing so, they tested God (see Exod. 17:2, 7)

Theirs was a one question quiz: *Did You bring us out here to let us die of thirst?* But they permitted God an extra credit question when they asked again: "Is the LORD among us or not?" (Exod. 17:7).

They clearly didn't expect a correct response. They thought they would fail both God and His spokesman!

But God's version of the events is remarkably different: "*I tested you* at the waters of Meribah"!

They thought themselves justified in testing God, yet were oblivious to the fact that He *was testing them*. The testers were being tested!

Guess who failed their test?

On both occasions, their failure was commemorated with the name Meribah, which means to strive, quarrel or contend.

Worship is not merely about our words to God—be they prayers, songs, acclimations, shouts of praise, verbal confession of sin or affirmations of faith. Worship is incomplete without God's Word to us! It was true of Joseph and it is true for us: "The word of the LORD tested him" (Ps. 105:19). We come to worship not simply to speak, but to hear.

Thus the preacher said, "Guard your steps when you go to the house of God. To draw near to listen is better than to offer the sacrifice of fools, for they do not know that they are doing evil. Be not rash with your mouth, nor let your heart be hasty to utter a word before God, for God is in heaven and you are on earth. Therefore let your words be few" (Eccles. 5:1–2).

When God's Word comes to us it is always a test of our faith. Every time God's Word is read and proclaimed the standing questions are: Will I believe Him or not? Will I prove my faith by obeying what He says?

We also observe here that *listening is a warning to heed*.

God cries out to His people:

> 8 Hear, O my people, while I admonish you!
> O Israel, if you would but listen to me!
>
> 9 There shall be no strange god among you;
> you shall not bow down to a foreign god.

God's Word fulfills many functions in our lives, but one primary function is that it admonishes us. The English word "admonish" is the translation of a Hebrew phrase that can be literally rendered, "I will testify against you."

This is precisely what God's Word does: "For the word of God is living and active, sharper than any two-edged sword, piercing to the division of soul and of spirit, of joints and of marrow, and discerning the thoughts and intentions of the heart" (Heb. 4:12).

Scripture does not flatter; it lays bare reality—not only about God, the world and others, but about you.

Scripture is like the unflattering photo someone snaps of you. You protest, *Oh my word! Is that what I really look like?*

Your brain quickly goes to work, rationalizing and concluding, *No! They just caught me at a bad angle. The lighting was all wrong!* Quickly you rifle through your files and find that one shot that caught you looking twenty pounds lighter and ten years younger than you really are. That picture instantly becomes your online profile picture.

But God's Word won't let us get away with such rationalization for long, for it admonishes us until we concede the realities it reveals about us.

We also discover that *listening is a promise to believe.*

Do you see here the generous nature of God extended in undeserved promises?

> 10 I am the LORD your God,
> who brought you up out of the land of Egypt.
> Open your mouth wide, and I will fill it.
>
> 14 I would soon subdue their enemies
> and turn my hand against their foes.
>
> 15 Those who hate the LORD would cringe toward him,
> and their fate would last forever.
>
> 16 But he would feed you with the finest of the wheat,
> and with honey from the rock I would satisfy you.

As unflattering as the Word of God can be to us personally, it holds before us a beautiful picture of what may be if we will truly hear and heed what He says to us.

A skeptic asks, "Are you saying God offers us the perfect life?"

Yes! Absolutely.

Realize that it won't all be delivered at the present moment—but that which is provided you now by God is the real deal, of the very same substance of that which will eventually be yours in fullest measure. Eternal life—*right now!* And on and on it will go, ever more fully, right through eternity.

This is what God spoke to the Israelites at Mount Sinai. Then He administered the test—by taking them into the wilderness to see if they'd believe Him or not.

Sadly, they opted for *not*.

Across the top of their test paper, in essence, God wrote: "Meribah" (strive quarel, or contend).

The test is always: "Will you believe me for My promises in Your life?"

The warning is: "Don't make me show you what you'll look like with all My grace sucked out of Your face!"

So you can see that listening to God's Word is *a watershed to divide*.

What does it mean to "listen" to God's Word? To "hear" Him?

In biblical terms: listen = obey. True hearing is demonstrated through acting upon what has been said.

In God's estimation, when they "did not listen to my voice" it was the same as their saying they "would not submit to me" (Ps. 81:11). He demands that to "listen to me" is to "walk in my ways" (81:13).

Thus, when God speaks we each have two choices, and only two. Delay is not one of them. To delay is to decide for unbelief, independence and disobedience. To delay is to fail the test without even picking up your pencil.

The test of God's Word is multiple choice—and there are only two choices: to believe and prove it by our obedience or to disbelieve and refuse to obey.

All else is sham, rationalization and game playing. God sees through it, even if we don't.

What is at stake when God's Word is opened—either by our hands or by the voice of another?

Forgiveness or fault! Time and eternity! Heaven and hell!

A failure to listen to God results in our being given "over to [our] stubborn hearts." When we fail to listen to and obey God, we have become those who "follow their own counsels" (Ps. 81:12).

Throughout World War II the United States relied upon a bomber known as *Lady Be Good*. It had a well-trained, much-experienced crew. They were bright and prepared for combat. Late one night, after another successful bombing run, they were returning to their base. They had made this flight many times. They knew how long it should have taken them to return.

But, unbeknownst to them, a strong tailwind kicked up and moved them much more quickly to their destination. They gazed in amazement at their instruments which accurately relayed the need for them to land the plane.

The crew, however, refused to heed the instruments' call. They flew on—far, far from their home base, gazing hopefully for some familiar pattern of lights.

Those lights never appeared.

Eventually, the *Lady Be Good* ran out of fuel and hit the dry desert floor below. The entire crew perished.[5]

It was an unnecessary loss. But it was an inevitable loss, as long as they followed "their stubborn hearts" and listened to "their own counsels" (Ps. 81:12).

We have been given a set of instruments by which to travel this dark world. They are given as "a lamp to [our] feet and a light to [our] path" (119:105). They are "a lamp and . . . a light" and are "the way of life" (Prov. 6:23). In the pages of the New Testament "we have the [Old Testament] prophetic word more fully confirmed" and Peter demands that "you will do well to pay attention [to it] as to a lamp shining in a dark place, until the day dawns and the morning star rises in your hearts" (2 Pet. 1:19).

God's voice, in the pages of the Bible, is always a watershed. It divides and separates that which moves either toward forgiveness or guilt, life or death, heaven or hell.

Maybe by now you feel like a receptionist at a busy office—too many calls arriving at the same time! But if we answer both, we discover God's point here in Psalm 81.

What does the convergence of the calls "come and worship" and "come and listen" tell us? Just this: *If I am not listening, I have not been worshiping.* If I am not heeding, my praise has been empty. If I am not obeying, my sacrifice of praise is a cover for a rebellious heart.

It is odd that we so often miss this, because God has been blunt about it over the years:

- "To obey is better than sacrifice" (1 Sam. 15:22).
- "The sacrifices of God are a broken spirit; a broken and contrite heart, O God, you will not despise" (Ps. 51:17).
- "To do righteousness and justice is more acceptable to the Lord than sacrifice" (Prov. 21:3).
- "For in the day that I brought them out of the land of Egypt, I did not speak to your fathers or command

> them concerning burnt offerings and sacrifices. But this command I gave them: 'Obey my voice, and I will be your God, and you shall be my people. And walk in all the way that I command you, that it may be well with you'" (Jer. 7:22–23).

Long ago God established His point: "I desire steadfast love and not sacrifice, the knowledge of God rather than burnt offerings" (Hos. 6:6).

James Montgomery Boice, longtime pastor of the historic Tenth Presbyterian Church in Philadelphia, pictured the average worship service—"What a strange anomaly: a happy, joyfully worshiping congregation and a neglected and offended God."[6] That sagacious commentator Derek Kidner put it succinctly, "God looks for listeners as well as singers."[7]

God issues two calls to us as His people: Come and worship! Come and Listen!

They must be answered together.

If you don't worship, you prove you haven't really heard and heeded the message of God's grace. For, once you taste of God's grace, worship will be your glad response.

If you don't listen, you prove you haven't really been worshiping. The answer is not to stop worshiping God. It is, rather, to stop using worship as a smoke screen to hide the reality of your heart.

The answer is to start listening—hearing and heeding God's Word—and offering Him the worship of an obedient life. This is the only "spiritual worship" that really counts with God (Rom. 12:1).

Worship in Action

- Take stock of how well you've been listening to God.
- Write out a prayer to God, asking Him to search you and to show you the truth about your hearing and heeding His voice in Scripture.
- Using Psalm 81 as your guide, ask yourself these questions as you read or hear God's Word:
    - What grace am I forgetting? (verses 6–7)
    - What word am I forgetting? (verse 7)
    - What word am I resisting? (verses 7–8)
    - What foreign word am I heeding? (verse 9)
    - What promise am I ignoring? (verses 10, 16)
    - What obedience am I withholding? (verse 11)
    - What self-deception am I embracing? (verse 12)

12

Living a Life of Accountability

Psalm 82

Take a moment and sort this list of words into two affinity groups. Mark on the page, write in the margin, use a separate sheet of paper or line it out mentally. In any case, divide these up into two groups of kindred ideas.

Worship	Courtroom
Judge	Sanctuary
Music	Indictment
Attorney	Temple
Praise	Prosecutor
Thanksgiving	Defense
Litigation	Prayer
Safety	Fear
Judicial	Adjudication
Deposition	Evidence

Okay, you've got your two groups. Now, let me ask: Which of those two lists sounds more like worship? We worship in the real world. We begin with worship—with God rightly considered and revered—and from there we discern reality. But life as worship is far from an ivory-tower experience.

Worship—pristine, pure, holy—must, for now, take place in the context of a dirty world.

This morning I feel a little dirty. As I write, we find ourselves in the midst of an election year. In fact, this precise moment finds us as a nation in the eye of the hurricane—the calm that is found in the few days between the national conventions of our two major political parties.

As I listen to each party's pundits and prophets, the words of the wise man come to mind: "The words of the wise heard in quiet are better than the shouting of a ruler among fools" (Eccles. 9:17). I wonder, what do we really learn from the conventions, other than who has best mastered the art of propaganda, posturing, spin and staging? And it's not just the conventions. It is the political ads engulfing TV, radio, billboards, Internet pop-ups and every other conceivable means of delivery.

As I hear and see the flood of rhetoric, I find myself wondering: *What of the unemployed, undefended, unrepresented and unprotected?*

The people too often become "talking points" for a candidate in an attempt at sensational leverage against his opponent. But at the end of the campaign season, at the end of the election cycle, at the end of the term, the people are routinely left unemployed, undefended, unrepresented and unprotected.

What does God think of this? And what does all this have to do with worship?

Psalm 82 provides the answer. Everything that takes place at the Republican National Convention will be brought into judgment. Everything that happens at the Democratic National Convention will be brought into judgment. Every ruler, politician, judge or person of influence—all the movers and shakers, all the power people of the world will be brought into judgment.

Strangely, this psalm of worship is not set in a sanctuary, but a courtroom.[1] God convenes His court to try the power people of the world.

The sterile walls of a courtroom may seem an odd place for worship. But before the trial ends and the verdict is handed down, Asaph will have guided us once again before the throne of God and invited us to kneel at His feet. By then we'll understand better how worship looks in a dirty world.

The Court Is Convened

> 1 God has taken his place in the divine council;
> in the midst of the gods he holds judgment.

The Judge has entered His court. More literally, "God *stands* in divine council." That is to say, God strides in to His courtroom and "takes His stand" (NASB).

The scene is much like what takes place in every courtroom across our land. The plaintiff and the defendant, along with their legal counsel, have gathered. The gallery is filled with onlookers. Suddenly a hinge squeaks, a door behind the bench moves and the bailiff raises his voice, "All rise!"

Indeed, all do rise.

> Men will go into caves of the rocks
> And into holes of the ground
> Before the terror of the LORD
> And the splendor of His majesty,
> When He arises to make the earth tremble.
>
> (Isa. 2:19, NASB)

Who is this Judge?

He is *Elohim*—"God" (Ps. 82:1, 8). The title designates God in His power. It pictures God as Creator.[2] The fourth word of our English Bibles depicts Him this way: "In the beginning, God [*Elohim*] created . . ." (Gen. 1:1).

He is also called *Elyon*, "the Most High" (Ps. 82:6). This title designates God as the "Highest" One.[3] The architecture of courtrooms may vary in many ways, but the judge's chair always sits higher than any other point in the court. No one stands taller than God in this court.

What is this court?

It is "the divine council." Rendered more literally, the line reads this way: "*Elohim* takes His stand in the assembly of the *El*." Remember, *El* or *Elohim* signifies strength.[4] As you can readily see, some form of *El* is used twice. The first designates God Himself, picturing Him in His power. But of whom does the second speak?

The phrase "in the midst of the gods [*El*]" has long proven a challenge to interpret and translate. There are three basic views of who is being referred to here. The first views this as a reference to Canaanite gods. This seems unlikely, however, because the Bible is clear that there really are no other gods (see Isa. 41:24; Acts 19:26; 1 Cor. 8:4; 10:19). They are nonentities: nothing more than wood, stone or metal—or a picture in someone's head or a desire in someone's heart. There is no actual being, except for the demonic spirits who deceive and delude those who lay down their lives in worship to those so-called gods (see 1 Cor. 10:20).

A second option views these as angels in heaven. It is true that sometimes angels seem to be referred to as the sons of God (see Job 1:6; 2:1), even as the present people are (see Ps. 82:6).

This too, however, seems unlikely because we have no evidence that angels "die like men" (Ps. 82:7, NASB).

A third possibility sees "gods" as a reference to earthly rulers or judges. This seems the more likely option because Jesus Himself quotes verse 6 in reference to human beings (see John 10:34–35). True, some argue against this because if they are men, then how can they die *like* men? But that is precisely the point! These power people do not think themselves "*mere* mortals" (82:7, NIV). Sure, they know they are human. Yet they fancy themselves above all that—invincible, unimpeachable, unable to be called to account!

The second, abbreviated form (*El*) does not speak of God, but of those granted by God (who alone possesses all authority in heaven and earth) a measured authority to rule at a particular time, in a particular place and over a particular people. These are people so blessed they might be tempted to "play god."

It is easy for us to get worked up over politicians getting theirs. So we need to think carefully about our application. We too are prone to selfishness, even (and maybe especially) in our application of the Bible. Yes, this does teach us that politicians, judges and power people will face God's judgment. They have received an appointment by God, and they will answer to God for how they have used the authority and influence He has vested in them. Whatever the political process may be, at the end of the day it is God who sets rulers in their place (see Rom. 13:1–7).

Such authority, clout and influence are a grace God gives to some, as He sovereignly sees fit. We often think of grace as relating to matters of salvation and spiritual need. And indeed it does, but there is, as we have already noted, such a thing as common grace. God makes the sun to shine and the rain to fall upon the just and the unjust alike (see Matt. 5:45). Those still separated from God by their sins often enjoy good food and happy relationships. In this they are graced by God.

The same is true of whatever position and power they may hold in life. Common grace, like saving grace, is free. But having received it, we are responsible for what we do with it. All grace is free, but no grace is accountability-free.

So ask yourself: *In what way has God graced me with position, power or influence?*

Realize that if you are a parent, spouse, employee, teacher, leader, manager, Christian or pastor, you qualify as a power person.

Doesn't this apply to "them"? Yes, of course, but to stop there is too self-serving. We each must make application to ourselves. How am I using my God-given position, influence and power? To what end? To whose advantage? For whose glory?

My guess is that the percentage of people reading this book who would identify themselves as power people is pretty small—perhaps infinitesimal to nonexistent.

But we each need to stop and see that God convenes His court and "holds judgment." He summons us all—you, me, us . . . and all our leaders.

"All rise!"

The Judge of all the earth summons all creation to sit as witnesses while He enters His court and renders judgment on those to whom He has given some measure of influence, authority, power and leadership.

The Indictment Is Read

The Judge reads the indictment against those in the docket. He indicts power people on two counts. Can you identify them?

> 2 How long will you judge unjustly
> and show partiality to the wicked?

In this day of instant information, no sooner has the politician concluded his speech than the fact-checkers go to work. Instantly we are told whether the speaker has overstated his case, twisted the facts or massaged the truth. It's a good thing, I suppose. But have you ever wondered: *Who checks the fact-checkers? Who monitors the bent of their analysis? Who assays whether objectivity has given way to political pandering?*

The Judge announces the first charge: *You have used your privilege to work injustice.* "How long will you judge unjustly" (Ps. 82:2)? The balance in their hand is predisposed to one side: toward special interest groups, ingratiating cronies and significant campaign donors. In politics, money often tips the scales of justice. And don't think for a minute that political pressures aren't exerting themselves within your local church, civic club or service organization.

Now the second charge: *You have used your privilege to favor the wicked.* "How long will you . . . show partiality to the wicked?" (82:2). *Green-justice* is not justice. "The wicked accepts a bribe in secret to pervert the ways of justice" (Prov. 17:23).

The Judge then lists the legal statutes which have been violated.

> 3 Give justice to the weak and the fatherless;
> maintain the right of the afflicted and the destitute.

> 4 Rescue the weak and the needy;
> deliver them from the hand of the wicked.

Privilege and position are given to protect "the weak" through justice, for they possess no power to overcome; "the fatherless," for they have no refuge into which they may run; "the afflicted," for they can find no healing; "the destitute," for they have no resources upon which to rely; and "the needy," for there are no reserves into which they may dip when in duress. Privilege and position are given that we might protect such people from "the hand of the wicked"(see Ps. 82:3–4).

Instead of aiding them, says the Judge, you have trampled them. You have climbed to your lofty position of advantage upon the stooped shoulders and weary backs of those less fortunate than yourself.

National borders can't hold back the sin nature endemic to all humans. Corruption needs no visa. Even as our most recent political process was playing out, the political machinery in Russia was grinding along. Opposition party members charged Russian leader Vladimir Putin with spending billions of tax payer's rubles on twenty lush residences, forty-three jets and four yachts. A former deputy prime minister estimated that maintenance alone on the Putin residences, jets and cars costs the Russian people 2.5 billion dollars a year. It was reported that Putin owned an exquisite collection of wristwatches worth 700,000 dollars. His nemesis Nemtsov claimed Putin has been "mistaking government property for his own" for years now.[5]

God indicts such selfishness wherever He finds it.

The Verdict Is Announced

> 5 They have neither knowledge nor understanding,
> they walk about in darkness;
> all the foundations of the earth are shaken.

There is debate among scholars concerning of whom the psalmist speaks. Does "they" refer to the power people or those they have abused? It seems more likely that it references the powerful, but the result is that these descriptions are true also of those over whom they rule.

The verdict is twofold. First, the Judge announces: *You operate from a failed worldview.* Specifically, they "have neither knowledge or understanding."

The current, dominant worldview interprets reality from a *me-first* perspective. But even where the needs of the disadvantaged are considered, there is a difference of opinion on the nature of that need and how to meet it.

Dr. Louis Markos, professor of English at Houston Baptist University, outlines the origins of the often-used tags "liberal" and "conservative." As originally conceived, a conservative was one who believed mankind to be morally corrupt and in need of the rule of law to keep him in the path of health, safety and progress. A liberal believed that man is basically good, but weighed down by ignorance and poverty. If only we can educate him and grant him resources, he will rise to be all he should be.[6]

Markos illustrates this through the writings of Charles Dickens. In *A Christmas Carol,* Ebenezer Scrooge is visited by the Ghost of Christmas Present. Within the folds of his robes, two children have taken refuge: a boy named Ignorance and a girl called Want. The spirit warns, "Beware them both, and all of their degree, but most of all beware this boy, for on his brow I see that written which is Doom, unless the writing be erased." Thus Dickens belies the worldview of the familiar Christmas tale.[7]

Whatever your label, or even if you defy all labels, apart from the redeeming grace of God through Christ your view of reality is askew. This can only be remedied by God's illuminating grace and the conformity of our minds to the written Word of God.

The second indictment is this: *You operate from a failed morality.* The Judge proclaims, you "walk about in darkness."

Morality arises from worldview. Worldview arises from theology. The order is fixed: theology – worldview – morality.

Realize that everyone is a theologian. Theology is a compound word comprised from the Greek words *theos* (God) and *logos* (word). Everyone has some thought about God and, if engaged, would speak those thoughts in words, however articulately or inarticulately. The question is not if you are a theologian, but if you are an *accurate* theologian.

Morality is an outgrowth of one's worldview.

One's worldview arises from one's theology.

One's theology arises from God's revelation—or more to the point, one's submission or lack of submission to that revelation.

God has revealed Himself through the world around us. It is like looking through an opaque pane of glass. Broad shapes and a basic outline can be discerned. From creation we are able to observe God's "invisible attributes, namely, his eternal power and divine nature." While the revelation through creation is not as detailed as we might wish, it is light enough to render us "without excuse" (see Rom. 1:20).

God has revealed Himself through the written Word of God, the Bible. This is precise, specific and clear. It is like looking at a personal letter printed in high resolution clarity. This is light enough to pierce "to the division of soul and of spirit, of joints and of marrow" and to lay bare "the thoughts and intentions of the heart" (Heb. 4:12).

God has supremely revealed Himself through the living Word of God, His Son, Jesus Christ. This revelation is living, upright and mobile. Here is the God of "eternal power and divine nature," having stepped to the other side of the pane of glass and now looking us in the eye. Here is the written Word standing upright and moving among us in the mess and confusion of life, showing us just what such a Word looks like when it stands upright and goes mobile among the peoples of the earth. Here we are confronted with "the light of the knowledge of the glory of God in the face of Jesus Christ" (2 Cor. 4:6).

If you begin with man, your morality of necessity will be earthbound, changing and "discovered" as you experience life and encounter its challenges. Such a morality will arise from the moment, from within you, and will be malleable according to the whims of your experiences and your feelings about those experiences.

Recently, I read of a judge in Brazil who performed a ceremony to form a "civil union" among three people—two women and a man. This is, to a growing percentage of the world's population, a perfectly legitimate step. For they have rejected the notion of a transcendent God who is revealed in the person of Jesus Christ and His written Word. They deny that this Word has authority over us today. Thus, in the current cultural climate, if three people want to be "married," so be it! Who are we to judge? The line of logic from one man with one woman in the bonds of holy matrimony for life to two women and a man as a convenient and civilly blessed union launches us on a trajectory into a world where marriage and family will mean anything an individual wishes it to mean.

The issue is fundamentally a theological one, for, having embraced certain thoughts about God, they have adopted a particular worldview and that worldview directs moral choices.

If, on the other hand, you begin with God, your morality will be transcendent, fixed and "delivered." The fulcrum of such a morality sits outside of one's experiences and feelings. It moves one's choices according to that external, fixed point of moral leverage. Such a morality sits in judgment of one's thoughts, motives, attitudes, words and actions.

Such a morality has specific implications regarding what constitutes a marriage/family, the basic building block of a healthy society.

Begin with a naturalistic view of the world and you have not only chosen to define your own terms, you have taken a sledgehammer to the very foundations of society and culture as designed and delivered by God. Thus Asaph cries, "All the foundations of the earth are shaken" (Ps. 82:5)! And "if the foundations are destroyed, what can the righteous do?" (Ps. 11:3).

Well, several things actually. We can repent. We can pray. We can vote (if you reside in a nation where that liberty is afforded you). We can hope—in something other than our politicians, parties and policies.

The Sentence Is Handed Down

6 I said, "You are gods,
sons of the Most High, all of you;

7 nevertheless, like men you shall die,
and fall like any prince."

Listen carefully to the words of the Judge as He hands down His sentence. First, He speaks of *a divine appointment.* He is emphatic in what He states—in essence saying, "It was *I* who said, 'You are gods.'"[8]

God gives to each her station in life, the role she fulfills, the authority, influence and clout that she wields. Such power is given by divine appointment. And with divine grace comes divinely imposed accountability. Spider-Man's uncle was correct: "With great power comes great responsibility."

The power people's misuse of that grace moved God to hand down a death sentence: "Like men you shall die, and fall like any prince" (Ps. 82:7).

Privilege does not deliver in the day of judgment. Great privilege has many benefits; immunity from prosecution is not one of them. In fact such grace heightens responsibility (see James 3:1).

Note the word "nevertheless" (Ps. 82:7). Despite your position, privilege and power, God must condemn you! Your privilege and power and position cannot deliver you now.

Not long ago the president of the United States of America quoted the vice president of the United States, saying "Don't judge me against the Almighty, judge me against the alternative."[9]

With all due respect, Mr. President, that is an option not left to any of us.

Recently, I was sobered as I watched a video of a news story. Tony Farmer was a high school senior in a nearby community. He was also a top one hundred basketball recruit. Major colleges fawned over him, vying for his commitment to their athletic program. Sadly, Tony Farmer was also an abuser. Security camera footage recorded him viciously beating his girlfriend. The video surfaced, he was indicted and convicted.

I watched the video of his sentencing. There he stood—young, powerful, a true specimen of youth, power and possibility—clad now in his orange jumpsuit, shackles around his wrists, flanked by a law enforcement officer, though inside the courtroom. At his other side was his attorney. The judge methodically read each charge against him, following it with the sentence she was imposing for his conviction. With each sentence announced, Tony turned to look at his attorney with a pleading look. Gone was the smug expression of invincibility.

One by one the years began to pile up. Tony's beseeching looks and whispered pleadings to his attorney became increasingly more desperate with each verdict and sentence. Eventually, realizing that the next seven years of his life were gone—and with them any dream of basketball stardom and financial gain—Tony collapsed to the floor, the courtroom filled with the sound of his weeping and wailing as he faced the gravity of his new reality.[10]

It is one of the most sobering things I've seen in a long time.

And well it ought to be. Jesus warned us repeatedly of a place characterized by "weeping and gnashing of teeth."

Note the effect this current conviction and sentencing is to have upon we who sit in the gallery:

> 8 Arise, O God, judge the earth;
> for you shall inherit all the nations!

The prayer voices the awareness that we're never going to get perfect justice from the peoples of this earth. The system will always be flawed. Among the power people, there will always be some who are selfish and corrupt. Perfect justice, vindication, equity and peace await the arrival of the all-powerful, eternally righteous Judge.

The Bible tells us there are three prongs to God's justice.

There is *the justice God meted out at the cross*. God the Father judged our sin in His Son on the cross. "God put [Jesus] forward [on the cross] as a propitiation [the satisfaction of His just and holy wrath against sin] by his blood [shed in death for us]" (Rom. 3:25). "The LORD has laid on him the iniquity of us all" (Isa. 53:6). God, "to deal with sin . . . condemned [judged] sin in the flesh" of His Son Jesus (Rom. 8:3, NRSV). "For our sake he [God the Father] made him [Jesus] to be sin who knew no sin, so that in him we might become the righteousness of God" (2 Cor. 5:21). This is precisely why "if we confess our sins, he is faithful and just to forgive us our sins and to cleanse us from all unrighteousness" (1 John 1:9). Because God the Father has already judged our sins in His Son, our substitute, it is not simply compassionate and merciful for Him to forgive our sins (though it is that as well). It is "faithful and just" for Him to forgive us, for if He judged them in His Son and then decided to judge them again in we who have fled in faith to His Son, He would be unjust in His condemnation. God works this way because "it was to show his righteousness at the present time, so that he might be just and the justifier of the one who has faith in Jesus" (Rom. 3:26).

There is also *the justice God will live out on the earth*. After Jesus returns, He will rule the earth for a thousand years (see Rev. 20:1–6). Upon the earth He will establish His perfect Kingdom. It will be a period of righteousness, peace and perfect justice, as Jesus Himself rules the nations (see Isa. 2:2–4). The Father invited His Son, saying "Ask of me, and I will make the nations your heritage, and the ends of the earth your possession" (Ps. 2:8). And they will be granted to Him. Jesus taught us to pray, "Your kingdom come, your will be done, on earth as it is in heaven" (Matt. 6:10). And indeed it will be.

Then there will be *the justice God metes out in the end.* Even in an earthly kingdom of perfect righteousness, ruled by our perfect King, a rebellion will arise (see Rev. 20:7–10). At that time, God will finally and forever judge and render inoperative the evil one and his hordes. Then God will summon all before His great white throne for judgment.

> Then I saw a great white throne and him who was seated on it. From his presence earth and sky fled away, and no place was found for them. And I saw the dead, great and small, standing before the throne, and books were opened. Then another book was opened, which is the book of life. And the dead were judged by what was written in the books, according to what they had done. And the sea gave up the dead who were in it, Death and Hades gave up the dead who were in them, and they were judged, each one of them, according to what they had done. Then Death and Hades were thrown into the lake of fire. This is the second death, the lake of fire. And if anyone's name was not found written in the book of life, he was thrown into the lake of fire. (Rev. 20:11–15)

Finally, a new heaven and a new earth with a New Jerusalem (see Rev. 21) will be established. At last we'll enjoy our long, eternal draught from the River of Life (see 22:1–5). Little wonder that the Bible ends with the prayer, "Amen. Come, Lord Jesus!" (Rev. 22:20). Small wonder that the cry of the early church was, "Maranatha" (1 Cor. 16:22, KJV)—"Our Lord, come!" (ESV).

With everything in me, I urge you—believe and rest in the justice already meted out against your sins when they were laid upon Jesus at the cross, so that you might come to share in the rule of Jesus and avoid the wrath of God to be unleashed against injustice.

Worship in Action

- Begin your time with God in praise—exalting Him as "the Most High," extolling Him as the God of all power. Humble yourself under His mighty hand (see 1 Pet. 5:6).
- Ask God to help you understand just how He has entrusted to you influence, power, clout or authority. Write down these positions, relationships, assignments and opportunities as God brings them to mind.
- Ask God to search your heart and reveal to you how you have handled this responsibility (see Ps. 139:23–24). Are there ways in which you have failed to reflect His justice in your dealings with others? Have you in any way favored the undeserving or overlooked the needy?
- Bow yourself afresh before God, taking refuge again in the fact that He has already satisfied His justice against your sin by judging it in Jesus. Pray back to God the Scriptures outlined at the end of this chapter, thanking Him for His forgiveness of these specific sins and failures.
- Complete your time of worship by expressing to God your longing for the arrival of His Kingdom of perfect righteousness. Tell Him of your longing

to be released from the power and presence of sin. Praise Him that His justice will right every wrong, heal every wound, exalt the lowly, bring low the haughty and glorify Himself.

13

Living a Life of Purpose

Psalm 83

Life doesn't just happen. Time will pass without your effort, but life requires intentionality. Presume upon life and you'll be looking up at it from a deep hole. The trouble is living *on purpose* is not easy. Intentionality increases the degree of difficulty dramatically. Stick the landing on this one and you're a champ. What is it about intentionality that complicates life?

Living life on purpose is difficult because panic keeps getting in the way. Mark it down: *Panic is the enemy of purpose.* Panic grabs *the immediate* by the hand and, by the sheer force of fear, drags it to the front of the line, prioritizing it before *the ultimate.* The immediate too often trumps the ultimate, and it's fear's fault.

What produces such panic? From where does fear arise? Often it is the incessant whispers of "What if?" that wear away at the foundation of life's purpose. What if . . .

- we can't make the mortgage payment?
- my lab reports bear bad news?
- my spouse stops loving me?
- my kids walk away from God?

- my boss gives me a pink slip?
- the car, the washing machine and the air conditioner all break down at the same time?
- the economy collapses?
- I lose my retirement accounts?
- the country falls apart?

Clearly, fear is the enemy of purpose. Thing is, *we are called to live life on purpose*. God invests His grace in us to a particular end. What is that end?

Psalm 83, the last of Asaph's psalms, reminds us of our purpose and helps us disable the fear that keeps us from pursuing it. The psalm arises from a time when God's people were surrounded by an enemy intent upon their destruction. Panic was setting in; purpose was fading. Asaph's final song reminds us that facing down our fears and living life on purpose rests upon three pillars.

The Eyes of God

At times, we all wonder if God sees or cares about our circumstances. Don't we all occasionally feel surrounded and overwhelmed by life's demands and threats? We need assurance that God is aware of our situation. Asaph knew the feeling. That's why his song opens with a panicky prayer.

> 1 O God, do not keep silence;
> do not hold your peace or be still, O God!

Three quick, abrupt commands are issued toward heaven: "Do not keep silence." "Do not hold your peace." "Do not . . . be still." The terms vary only for stylistic purposes—they communicate the same idea. One commentator suggests this paraphrase: "O God, don't be silent, don't be silent, don't be silent!"[1]

It sounds like the panicky caller, having just dialed 911, fearfully repeating, "Please pick up! Please pick up! Please pick up!" It is like the frightened child hiding in the basement from the tornado thundering down upon her home—hands over her ears, curled into a ball, rocking back and forth, dwarfed by the train-like roar of the twister and crying out, "O God, please! Please, O God, please!"

In other words: "God, *do* something!" It is not so much a request for God to clear His throat and speak, but to rise and act. It is based on the apparent nonresponse of God. Does He know? Is He aware? Does He care? "Hey God, in case You missed the newsfeed at the bottom of Your screen, we're in big trouble down here!"

And not only is there panic, *there is a plot feeding the panic!*

> 2 For behold, your enemies make an uproar;
> those who hate you have raised their heads.

These enemies "make an uproar" against God's people. The same expression is used to describe the waves of the sea that "roar and foam" (Ps. 46:3). It is not the sound of gentle lapping at the edge of a pond, nor is it the soothing, rhythmic waves washing over a sandy beach. It is a dark, rocky coastline with angry breakers threatening to tear the land from its moorings.

These foes "have raised their heads." This phrase depicts an act arising from a heart of self-confidence and overt hostility.[2]

They are plotting a conspiracy.

> 3 They lay crafty plans against your people;
> they consult together against your treasured ones.

O God, we are "your people . . . your treasured ones"! The word *treasured* has the nuance of "hidden," (KJV) as in valued ("treasured") or protected ("sheltered," NKJV). Or perhaps it includes both. You protect something because you value it! You guard your eyes because you value your eyesight.

We are, O God, the one's You've promised to care for as "the apple of [your] eye" (Deut. 32:10). Have You not said, O Lord, that "he who touches you touches the apple of his eye" (Zech. 2:8)?

> 4 They say, "Come, let us wipe them out as a nation;
> let the name of Israel be remembered no more!"

The panic didn't arise from an inconvenience that delayed their plans or rewrote their schedule. They faced the threat of utter extinction. This was real, justifiable fear.

Isn't this a threat the Jews have faced time and again throughout their history? In that dark hole of history between the Old and New Testaments, Antiochus Epiphanes sought annihilation of the Jewish people. In AD 70, the Roman general Titus marched on Jerusalem, destroying the city, killing and dispersing its citizens. Anti-Semitism has continued through the ages. In Russia, between 1918 and 1921, 100,000 to 150,000 Jews were killed.[3] When Adolph Hitler became chancellor of Germany in 1933, the ominous signs hung heavy in the air. He oversaw the extermination of some six million Jews between 1938 and 1945.[4]

Drawing up to the time of the Six-Day War of 1967, Arab and Muslim leaders repeatedly called for Israel's annihilation. President Nasser of Egypt declared, "We aim at the destruction of the State of Israel." President Abdel-Rahman Aref of Iraq said, "The existence of Israel is an error which must be rectified . . . our goal is clear—to wipe Israel off the map." Ahmad Shukairy, chairman of the Palestine Liberation Organization, warned, "We shall destroy Israel and its inhabitants." Syrian Defense Minister Hafez Assad said, "I as a military man, believe that the time has come to enter into a battle of annihilation."[5]

These sentiments are not relics of a bygone age. It is truer now than ever. The news is filled with vitriolic demands for the annihilation of Israel. Not long ago, the Ayatollah Ali Khamenei of Iran called for the removal of "this corrupting material" (by which he meant the Jews and their nation, Israel). He declared that Iran has a " 'jurisprudential justification' to kill all the Jews and annihilate Israel."[6] While Iran's vice president, Mohammad-Reza Rahimi made a rabidly anti-Semitic speech at an international antidrug conference being held in Tehran—in which he blamed Jews for the worldwide drug trade.[7] And President Mahmoud Ahmadinejad went on record declaring, "Any freedom lover and justice-seeker in the world must do its best for the annihilation of the Zionist regime in order to pave the path for the establishment of justice and freedom in the world."[8]

At the end of time, this hatred, fury and rage will find its crescendo in the Antichrist who will pour out his murderous bile upon all followers of the true God.

Asaph invites us to *picture the encircling doom*. The heart of the psalm provides a list of the conspirators. Note the ten nations that united to encircle God's people and defeat her.

> 5 For they conspire with one accord;
> against you they make a covenant—
>
> 6 the tents of Edom and the Ishmaelites,
> Moab and the Hagrites,

7 Gebal and Ammon and Amalek,
Philistia with the inhabitants of Tyre;
8 Asshur also has joined them;
they are the strong arm of the children of Lot. *Selah*

Locate these nations on a map of the ancient world and notice they surrounded the Promised Land on three sides—north, east and south. With the Mediterranean Sea to the west this meant that God's people were getting the squeeze. And it was a death lock around the throat!

It reminds me of the words of King Hussein of Jordan, after he signed a pact with Egypt on May 30, 1967. He said, "All of the Arab armies now surround Israel. The UAR, Iraq, Jordan, Yemen, Lebanon, Algeria, Sudan, and Kuwait."[9]

The year 1976 was not the first time Israel has been surrounded and it won't be the last. While it does not name these same ten nations, the Bible does hold before us a prophetic image of a ten-nation confederation that will arise in the last days and once again threaten Israel.

Daniel 7 records a vision God gave to His prophet, a vision of four beasts. The first represented Babylon; the second, the Medo-Persian Empire. The third depicted Greece; the fourth, the Roman Empire. But it seems that, at some point, the vision skips beyond the earthly, historic Roman Empire and looks upon the end of time and what some have called a revived Roman Empire. It depicts ten horns representing a new ten-nation confederation which will set its eyes upon the annihilation of Israel. Similarly, Revelation 17 also pictures ten kings coming together to war with God and His people.

These are not the same nations as recorded here in Psalm 83, but this does serve as a prophetic picture of the kind of thing the last days will bring forth. Throughout history, God's people have faced panic—fear fed by a plot to squeeze them into a mold of the world's making. It seems the world is never more unified than when opposing God and His people.

We have here in Psalm 83 both an ancient identification and a historical precedent. We've only begun to trace the connection. But rest assured there will be a prophetic, end-time fulfillment. Yet there must also be a present, personal application. And in this commentator Willem VanGemeren helps us. Among these ten nations in Psalm 83 he identifies three kinds of foes.[10]

First, are *the Troublers*. For Israel that included Edom, the Ishmaelites, Moab, the Hagrites, Ammon, Philistia and Amalek. These pesky nations were ever-present to exploit Israel's weaknesses, to snap at their heels, to rejoice over their failures.

Jesus spoke of seed that fell upon a well-beaten path. The path pictures a condition of the human heart. A constant barrage of feet has beaten the path hard. The seed of God's Word can't penetrate the heart. Seed lies vulnerable upon the hardened path. An evil one comes to steal away the seed before it can sprout (see Matt. 13:3–4, 19).

In our own struggles, this pictures our battle against the flesh. Our sinful nature troubles us again and again, wooing us down the old familiar trail of besetting sins.

Second, there are *the Seducers*. For ancient Israel these included Gebal and Tyre. They threatened God's people by promoting enculturation. They sought not to destroy, but to seduce.

In Jesus' parable, some of the seed fell also among thorns. There the thorns grew and choked out the wheat of God's Word. Jesus said, "The cares of the world and the deceitfulness of riches choke the word, and it proves unfruitful" (Matt. 13:22).

For us the world system serves as a pervasive moral atmosphere which we breathe each second of every day. The gravity-like force of its downward pull—away from God and His ways—is constant and inescapable in this life. It wears at our standards and wearies us in our convictions.

Finally, there are *the Oppressors.* In Psalm 83 this role was played by Asshur, which probably refers to Assyria who defeated and exiled the northern kingdom of Israel.

Jesus' parable continues by speaking of seed that fell on rocky soil. It pictures the one who "receives it with joy, yet he has no root in himself, but endures for a while, and when tribulation or persecution arises on account of the word, immediately he falls away" (Matt. 13:20–21).

In our own battle, this alerts us to the devil who threatens, intimidates and deceives—all in an effort to make us back down and "live small."

The net effect of the troublers, seducers and oppressors is that we feel cut off, demoralized, surrounded—squeezed by this world into its mold. We begin to lose our way. Instead of living life on purpose, we live life for survival. Rather than life as worship, we live for self-preservation.

If we're going to live lives of purpose, we need to rest upon this first pillar—the eyes of God. True, we are surrounded like Israel was, but God sees and cares about us and our unique and individual plights. God is aware of you and me and all that threatens us.

One pillar, however, does not make a firm foundation. I need, then, to rest also upon God's hand.

The Hand of God

We not only wonder if God knows our plight, but question whether He will act on our behalf. Yes, I am concerned that God *see*, but will God *save*? I not only need assurance of God's care, I need evidence of God's action.

Thus Asaph prays, *God, act like You have in the past*!

As he prays, the psalmist recalls two of Israel's greatest victories. These two are selected because they epitomize God's deliverance of His undermanned, outgunned, overwhelmed people! Both come from the days of the judges.

> 9 Do to them as you did to Midian,
> as to Sisera and Jabin at the river Kishon,
>
> 10 who were destroyed at En-dor,
> who became dung for the ground.
>
> 11 Make their nobles like Oreb and Zeeb,
> all their princes like Zebah and Zalmunna,
>
> 12 who said, "Let us take possession for ourselves
> of the pastures of God."

What's that all about? I mean, that's all very interesting (and it's kind of fun to say "Zebah and Zalmunna" every once in a while), but what does that mean for us?

In answer, consider these two historical accounts.

First, we have the amazing account of Gideon leading God's people to victory over Midian (see Ps. 83:9–12). You'll find the historical record in Judges 6–8. For years the Israelites had been so cruelly beaten down by the Midianites that they hid in hills, caves and holes in the ground. In their distress they called out to God.

God responded by calling Gideon.

Gideon, however, wasn't exactly Chuck Norris! He was a timid, frightened man. Our first picture of him is as he is beating out wheat—down in a wine press (instead of high on a windswept hill) so the Midianites wouldn't find him.

But, fear or not, Gideon stepped forward and told of God's desire to deliver His people. His speech must not have gone badly for thirty-two thousand men came together to fight under his leadership.

But God spoke again to Gideon, saying he had too many soldiers.

So Gideon was directed to ask, "Who here is afraid to go to battle?" That thinned the ranks by twenty-two thousand.

But God said he still had far too many soldiers for the task. So, at God's bidding, Gideon called for a water break. Watching carefully, as directed by God, this reduced the military ranks of Israel by almost ten thousand more!

In the end, Gideon and just three hundred soldiers stood together to face 120,000 Midianites.

As crazy as God's enlistment scheme had seemed, His battle instructions appeared just as foolhardy. Their weapons? Trumpets, pitchers, torches. The plan? When God gave the sign, they were to shout, break the pitchers, wave their torches and sound the trumpets.

They obeyed and the Midianites flew into a panic, killing one another. Gideon and his men pursued Zebah and Zalmunna (see Ps. 83:11) and utterly defeated the remnant of Midian.

Clearly, God's people had not been delivered by a powerful leader, a wise plan or overwhelming troops and weaponry. They had been saved by the hand of God.

When we remember to take up God's purpose as our own and refuse to let panic push it into the background, we find that His eye is upon us and He moves on our behalf.

The second account Asaph recalls is that of Barak the warrior and Deborah the judge. They fought against Jabin, the king of Canaan, and Sisera, the commander of Jabin's armies (see Ps. 83:9). These men had oppressed God's people for twenty long years (see Judg. 4–5).

God's people cried out for relief. He had mercifully raised up Deborah to serve as the judge of Israel. In a patriarchal society, a woman in the leading office was a signal of just how weak the nation had become.

Deborah called upon Barak to gather ten thousand men and to fight against the armies of Jabin. Israel's ten thousand went up against a vast army. Mere foot soldiers stood before nine hundred iron chariots.

Yet, by the hand of God, the few defeated the many; the footed, the outfitted. When he saw the battle going against him, Commander Sisera abandoned his chariot and fled on foot. In his flight, he came to the tents of a woman named Jael. Sisera thought himself safe, for she and her people were at peace with his nation. But, hiding in her tent, he fell into a deep sleep. As he snoozed, she rummaged through the toolbox, pulling out a hammer and tent peg. One swing from Jael's womanly hand and mighty Sisera's earthly tent folded forever.

Pompous Jabin and mighty Sisera—both defeated at the hands of, *gulp*, women!

When God's people, though oppressed and weak, take up God's purpose, they find Him watchful of their plight and willing to move His hand on their behalf.

Psalm 83, of course, arose out of a particular problem. It grew out of a specific historical situation that befell a specific people at a specific time. We don't know exactly what that historical situation was. However, many agree that the closest parallel in Israel's recorded history was that of Jehoshaphat standing against a united coalition of Gentile nations (see 2 Chron. 20).

Jehoshaphat was a godly king. He had, however, an unwise predisposition toward wicked King Ahab of the northern kingdom of Israel. In fact, he had entered an alliance with Ahab. For this failure, God allowed a coalition of nations to come against Jehoshaphat—not a ten-nation confederation as in Psalm 83, but a three-nation union of Ammon, Moab and the Meunites.

Jehoshaphat heard of a "great multitude" marching upon him (2 Chron. 20:2) and, predictably, fell victim to fear. In his panic, he wisely called out to God. As the king prayed he recounted what God had done for His people in the past (see 20:7). He asked God to do the same in his day (see 20:12).

As Jehoshaphat called out to God, the Spirit of the Lord moved upon a Levite—who just happened to be numbered among "the sons of Asaph" (20:14). He stepped forward with a word from God, saying, "Do not be afraid and do not be dismayed at this great horde, for the battle is not yours but God's" (20:15).

In response, the king and all the citizens of his kingdom "fell down before the LORD, worshiping the LORD" (20:18).

Do you see it? In the midst of great panic, they reclaimed God's purpose for their lives!

The next morning, by faith, they marched out to the wilderness where the battle would be waged. Jehoshaphat set his battle plan, arranged his troops and then, defying all standard military wisdom, deployed the choir to the front of the line!

These marched into battle calling out: "Give thanks to the LORD, for his steadfast love endures forever" (2 Chron. 20:21).

The result was that "when they began to sing and praise, the LORD set an ambush against the men of Ammon, Moab, and Mount Seir, who had come against Judah, so that they were routed" (20:22)!

In the midst of panic, they reclaimed God's purpose. God's glory became their purpose; God's praise, their passion.

Everything about everything is about the glory of God. So, if in the face of forces and foes bigger than us, we focus upon God, making His praise our purpose, we can trust that God will care for what we are unable to deal with.

It is fitting that in the last of these psalms of Asaph we are brought full circle to this basic building block of our purpose.

Remembering God's record of faithfulness, Asaph prayed again, *God, act now in the present*!

God had moved, proving that when the weak make His purpose theirs, He acts on their behalf. But we need this to be present experience. So in this present distress, before these current enemies . . .

> 13 O my God, make them like whirling dust,
> like chaff before the wind.
>
> 14 As fire consumes the forest,
> as the flame sets the mountains ablaze,
>
> 15 so may you pursue them with your tempest
> and terrify them with your hurricane!

We too can reclaim our purpose, even in the face of justifiable panic. As we do, we are reminded that . . .

> When you're up against a struggle
> that shatters all your dreams
> And your hopes have been cruelly crushed
> by Satan's manifested schemes
> And you feel the urge within you
> to submit to earthly fears
> Don't let the faith you're standing in
> seem to disappear

Praise the Lord,
    He can work through those who praise Him
Praise the Lord,
    for our God inhabits praise
Praise the Lord,
    for the chains that seem to bind you
Serve only to remind you,
    that they drop powerless behind you
When you praise Him.[11]

Praise is a discipline that must be exercised with purpose. Panic has come to the back of the line, taken *the immediate* by the hand and, through sheer force of fear, dragged it to the front. There it looks *the ultimate* in the eye, commanding, "Find your place!" Fear demands, "All that matters is the 'now,' the panic, the fear, these circumstances." But the people of God say, "Yes, circumstances are real; but I also know my purpose." We don't deny the realities of life; we don't stick our heads in the sand. Nevertheless, our purpose is—even in the midst of these hard realities—to know that God *sees* and that He will *move His hand* if we will take up our purpose in life. Our purpose is His praise; our goal, His glory.

Living a life of purpose rests upon three pillars. We've thus far only seen two: God's all-seeing eyes and God's all-powerful hand. Before we close the book on life as worship, let me introduce to you the third foundation. Appropriately, it is in the final stanza of this final psalm of Asaph that it is explicit (see Ps. 83:16–18).

The Glory of God

Whatever the panic, whatever the troublers are plotting, whatever the seducers are saying, whatever the oppressors are threatening, whatever the problem may be, whatever circumstances have arisen—is God's glory my purpose?

Am I more concerned for God's glory than I am my escape from these circumstances?

We need desperately to be centered once again on our purpose. We must recommit to making our lives the stage upon which God's glory is promoted. I need a fresh commitment to honoring and reverencing God.

The psalmist first asks God to humble his enemies: "Fill their faces with shame" (Ps. 83:16). But this is not for mere vengeance or vindication. A higher purpose has laid hold of him—and must lay hold of us as well.

Notice that he prays, "Fill their faces with shame, that . . ." He is not simply praying for their humiliation. There is a specific purpose toward which he is praying, a purpose which cannot be realized in them without humility.

Humble them, "that they may seek your name, O LORD" (83:16).

Seeking "your name" is another way of saying, "seeking God's person." We must each know God as He in fact is—in all the terrors of infinite holiness, righteousness and justice; and in all the reassurances of divine mercy, grace and forgiveness.

The verb "seek" carries in it the idea of "require" or "desire."[12] You *require* something, so you seek it! A drowning man seeks (requires) a firm foothold. You *desire* something, so you seek it! A hungry man goes looking for (desires) food.

It is a prayer that says, "Lord, make them see how much they require Your intervention. Let them see themselves before You in Your glory! Make them desire what only You can provide." We will only pray this way for our foes when we confess that it's not all about me and my panic, but about God and His glory among all the peoples of the earth.

Derek Kidner is right when he says the psalmist "comes to the brink of praying for the enemy's conversion."[13]

But seeking is not the end. Knowing you need God is not the finish line. Knowing only He can meet your need is not the final destination. This is a must—but it is not the most.

Indeed, he prays not only that they might seek God but that they might ultimately know Him.

> 17 Let them be put to shame and dismayed forever;
> let them perish in disgrace,
>
> 18 that they may know that you alone,
> whose name is the LORD,
> are the Most High over all the earth.

To *know* is deeper than to *seek*. Seeking is required. It speaks of awareness of need and desire for that which alone can satisfy it. But knowing involves an acknowledgment, an admission that leads to an experience of the deepest, most personal kind possible.

We may be troubled by what sounds like vindictiveness in verses 16 and 17. But these statements must be balanced with the intercessions of verses 16 and 18. These requests make us realize: the prayer is that both those who oppose God's purpose and the people who seek to live according to that purpose may come to see the realities of truth and error, light and darkness, heaven and hell.

The heart of the prayer may be summarized in this way: "O Lord, show them the realities of who You are and who they are (and are not) before You. Reveal to them the provision of Your grace and forgiveness. Give them an opportunity to join in living for Your purpose. Grant that they may live life as worship."

And, ultimately, how has God made this opportunity available? Through Jesus Christ.

God wants everyone to know that all the shame, vengeance, wrath and judgment due to them for their stubborn, sinful independence from Him has already been meted out upon His Son as He hung on the cross. Your sin has already been judged—if you will be counted by faith as one who is "in Christ."

God extended His grace in this way—through Jesus—that all might seek and know Him. "Therefore God has highly exalted him and bestowed on him the name that is above every name, so that at the name of Jesus every knee should bow, in heaven and on earth and under the earth, and every tongue confess that Jesus Christ is Lord, *to the glory of God the Father*" (Phil. 2:9–11).

And therein is our purpose. Therein is the essence of life as worship: living moment by moment, day by day, in all life's complexities "to the glory of God." In this way, reality comes into sharper focus. Thus we gain a reverence-focused view of what actually "is."

We return to that purpose and gain that clarity as we rest upon the steady pillars of the knowledge of God's care (the eyes of God), His intervention on our behalf (the hand of God) and His preeminence over all things (the glory of God).

Life is full of pain and threats and fears. If, in the midst of it all, I am assured that God knows and cares, that He will act and that—through it all and at the end of it all—God will be glorified, then I can commit myself to my divinely given purpose. That purpose is to glorify Him. Or, put more simply, to live *life as worship*!

Worship in Action

- Prayerfully and honestly, take note of that which currently moves you toward panic and fear. Write these down.
- Before the Lord, process prayerfully the full realities of those threats. Be honest and authentic in expressing your fear to God.
- Now, by faith, thank God that He is fully aware of all those dangers and threats. Admit He knows them better than you do.
- Express your gratitude for God's faithfulness in the past in overcoming that which frightens you. Be specific. Draw upon the history of your walk with God.
- Ask God to act similarly in your current circumstances.
- As a closing act of worship, drawing upon all that we've learned along this journey, write out a prayer to God in which you sign your life and circumstances over to Him. Ask Him to use you and the circumstances of your life to promote His glory. Ask that He make your life a means of drawing others to live their lives as worship to the Lord.

Notes

Preface

1. For further reading along this line check out *Metaphors We Live By*, George Lakoff and Mark Johnson (Chicago: The University of Chicago Press, 1980).
2. See Warren W. Wiersbe's *Preaching and Teaching with Imagination* (Colorado Springs: Chariot Victor Books, 1994) for an enlightening study in the power of biblical metaphor and imagery.
3. See my book *Long Story Short* (Fort Washington: CLC Publications, 2010) where I develop these two themes from beginning to end, Genesis to Revelation.
4. Derek Kidner, *Proverbs* (Downers Grove: InterVarsity Press, 1964), 59.
5. Psalm 50 and Psalms 73–83 all begin with the prescript "of Asaph." The Hebrew word translated "of" is somewhat flexible in meaning and can indicate that the particular psalm was written *by* Asaph or perhaps that it was *for* or *in memory of* Asaph.

Chapter 1

1. Warren W. Wiersbe, ed., *The Best of A. W. Tozer* (Harrisburg: Christian Publications, Inc., 1978), 217.

2. John Calvin, *The Institutes of the Christian Religion* (Christian Classics Ethereal Library) 101, http://www.ccel.org/ccel/calvin/institutes.pdf.
3. Throughout the book I will make applications related to both worship as a gathered, corporate, formal experience as well as an individual, personal, life-flow affair. I will not entirely disconnect the two, but freely move back and forth suggesting applications to both. Asaph was both an individual worshiper and a leader of worshipers. The one flowed freely into the other as it must also in our lives today.
4. Francis Brown, S. R. Driver, and Charles A. Briggs, *The Brown-Driver-Briggs Hebrew and English Lexicon: With an Appendix Containing Biblical Aramaic* (Oxford: Clarendon, 1907), 63.
5. Wiersbe, *The Best of A.W. Tozer*, 217.
6. Gen. 46:11; Asaph of Gerhom (1 Chron. 6:39–43); Heman of Kohath (6:33–38); and Ethan of Marari (15:17).
7. You can tally it up for yourself in 1 Chronicles 15:4–10.
8. As we deal with each of the psalms of Asaph, I will at times speak of "Asaph" and at other times of "the sons of Asaph" in regard to authorship. I will not attempt to untangle the knotted problems related to the precise time or author of each psalm. Technical commentaries will aid you in this quest. As noted earlier, the Hebrew word translated "of" is somewhat flexible in meaning and can indicate that the particular psalm was written *by* Asaph or perhaps that it was *for* or *in memory of* Asaph.

9. Merrill F. Unger, *Unger's Bible Handbook* (Chicago: Moody Press, 1966), 212, 254.
10. Brown, Driver, and Briggs, 556.
11. *Popular Science* 97, no. 4, October 1920, . accessed January 24, 2015, http://books.google.com/books/about/Popular_Science.html?id=pykDAAAAMBAJ.
12. Merrill C. Tenney, ed., *The Zondervan Pictorial Encyclopedia of the Bible 4* (Grand Rapids: Zondervan Publishing House, 1975, 1976), 877.
13. Terry Wardle, *Untamed Christian, Unleashed Church: The Extravagance of the Holy Spirit in Life and Ministry* (Abilene: Leafwood Publishers, 2010).

Chapter 2

1. G.K. Chesterton, *Illustrated London News*, May 1928, accessed January 24, 2015, http://quoteinvestigator.com/2014/07/20/drawing/.
2. John Phillips, *Exploring Psalms* (Neptune, New Jersey: Loizeaux Brothers, 1988), 1:395–396.
3. *The Complete Biblical Library* – Psalms. Springfield, IL: World Library Press, Inc., 1996. WORD*search* CROSS e-book.
4. Allan Harman, *Psalms: A Mentor Commentary* (Inverness: Christian Focus Publications, 1999), 1:199.
5. James Montgomery Boice, *Psalms: An Expositional Commentary* (Grand Rapids: Baker Books, 1996), 2:419.
6. A. Attanasio in *A Manual of Guidelines, Quotations and Versatile Phrases for Basic Oral Communication*, ed. Xin-

An Lu and Hong Wang (Bloomington: iUniverse, Inc., 2003), 73.

7. Their real names shall remain hidden.
8. Phillips, *Exploring Psalms,* 1:402.
9. *The Avengers*, directed by Joss Whedon (Marvel Studios, 2012), Film.
10. A.W. Tozer, *The Knowledge of the Holy* (San Francisco: Harper & Row, Publishers, 1961), 1.

Chapter 3

1. E.V. Hill, sermon example heard by the author, unknown date.
2. Brown, Driver and Briggs, 1022.
3. There is some question as to precisely who is quoted in verses 10–11. If it is a further statement by the "wicked," it represents further mocking on their part, asking "Where is God? Where is this justice you talk about? I dare God to judge me!" If, on the other hand, it is a statement made by those stumbling in their faith, they are concluding that God may "know" what the wicked are doing, but He is too exalted, too lofty to be bothered with the mundane affairs of those struggling to honor Him on earth!
4. "Come on! Look! Take an honest assessment."
5. "German teen solves 300-year-old mathematical riddle posed by Sir Isaac Newton," *Fox News*, published May 27, 2012, http://www.foxnews.com/world/2012/05/27/german-teen-solves-300-year-old-mathematical-riddle-posed-by-sir-isaac-newton/.

6. Donald M. Williams, *The Preacher's Commentary: Psalms 73–150* (Nashville: Thomas Nelson Publishers, 1989), 19.
7. Malcom Muggeridge, "But Not of Christ," in *Seeing Through the Eye: Malcolm Muggeridge on Faith*, ed. Cecil Kuhne (San Francisco: Ignatius Press, 2005), 29–30.
8. Boice, *Psalms: An Expositional Commentary,* 2:614; John Goldingay, *Psalms: Psalms 42–89*, Baker Commentary on the Old Testament Wisdom and Psalms (Grand Rapids: Baker Academic, 2007), 2:418.

Chapter 4

1. *Merriam-Webster Online*, s.v. "lament," accessed January 24, 2015, http://www.merriam-webster.com/dictionary/lament.
2. Elisabeth Elliot, *A Chance to Die: The Life and Legacy of Amy Carmichael* (Grand Rapids: Fleming H. Revell, 1987), 333.
3. R.C. Sproul, *The Invisible Hand: Do All Things Really Work for Good?* (Dallas: Word Publishing, 1996), 97.
4. Unger, *Unger's Bible Handbook*, 239.
5. At the crossing of the Red Sea.
6. Perhaps a symbolic reference to Egypt: Does Leviathan refer to the crocodile (i.e., of the Nile)? Or is this a reference to mythical creatures of surrounding cultures, like Babylon, and declaring, "God, You are greater than them!"?
7. Providing water from the rock in the wilderness (see Exod. 17).

8. Dividing the Jordan and leading Joshua and the people through on dry ground (see Josh. 3–4).
9. John and Joanna Stumbo, *An Honest Look at a Mysterious Journey* (Fox Island: Nesting Tree Books, 2011).
10. This information was gathered from personal testimonies during a visit to Belarus by the author.

Chapter 5

1. Phillips, *Exploring Psalms*, 1:623.
2. Warren W. Wiersbe, *The Bible Exposition Commentary: Wisdom and Poetry* (Colorado Springs: Victor, 2004), 225.
3. Kidner, *Psalms 73–150*, 2:271.
4. See Psalm 7:15, 16; 9:15; 35:8; 57:6; 94:23; Proverbs. 5:22.
5. *The Complete Biblical Library – Psalms*. Springfield, IL: World Library Press, Inc., 1996. WORD*search* CROSS e-book.
6. Boice, *Psalms: An Expositional Commentary,* 2:629.
7. Kidner, *Psalms 73–150*, 2:273

Chapter 6

1. Dave Alsup, "Pilot's deadly in-flight heart attack threatens to renew age debate," CNN.com, September 27, 2013, http://www.cnn.com/2013/09/27/us/boise-airline-pilot-heart-attack/index.html?hpt=hp_t2.
2. John Kitchen, *Long Story Short* (Fort Washington: CLC Publications, 2010), 107.

3. E.g., Boice, *Psalms: An Expositional Commentary,* 2:633; Harman, *Psalms: A Mentor Commentary*, 1:264; Kidner, *Psalms 73–150*, 2:274.
4. OMF International, accessed 12/15/14, http://omf.org/us/archives/vietnam/.

Chapter 7

1. And what is meditating but *intentional* remembering? The Hebrew word means to rehearse, repeat or roll something over and over again in one's mind. Gary G. Cohen, "שִׂיחַ (*siah*)," Theological Word Book of the Old Testament (Chicago: Moody Press, 1980), 2:875-876.
2. Brown, Driver, and Briggs, 242.
3. Carl Philip Webber, "הָמָה (*hāmâ*)," *Theological Wordbook of the Old Testament* (Chicago: Moody Press, 1980), 1:219.
4. *Get Low*, directed by Aaron Schneider (K5 International, 2009), Film.
5. There are four basic options: 1) It could be rendered as the English Standard Version presents it: "I will appeal to this, to the years of the right hand of the Most High." That is to say, my hope is that the God who has been so good, generous, gracious and kind in the past, will behave similarly in the future. This is a good and valid hope and is a perspective the Bible holds out to us in other places. 2) It could also be rendered as it is presented in the margin of the English Standard Version: "This is my grief: that the right hand of the Most High has changed." That is to say, what causes me pain is that God no longer seems to be dealing with me in grace as He has in my

past experience. I have no precedence in my experience for this kind of behavior from God. 3) It could mean: "I will appeal to this, that the right hand of the Most High has changed." The idea then would be, my hope is that the God who in the past was so gracious and generous with His blessings (but appears to have changed at the present) perhaps will change His course yet again and send us grace and blessings. 4) A final possibility is this rendering: "This is my grief: the years of the right hand of the Most High." The idea would be: This is what causes me pain—that God seems, according to my present situation, to have changed from His gracious, benevolent self. See Boice, *Psalms: An Expositional Commentary*, 2:641.

6. All these occurrences are according to the ESV text; See Boice, *Psalms: An Expositional Commentary*, 2:638; Kidner, *Psalms 73–150*, 2:277.
7. Robertson McQuilkin, "Therapeutic Theology for Hurting People," accessed January 24, 2015, http://www.ciu.edu/faculty-publications/article/therapeutic-theology-hurting-people.

Chapter 8

1. Psalm 78 is unique in a couple of ways: 1) It is the second longest of the psalms, second only to Psalm 119; and 2) In this psalm Asaph does not speak directly to God; rather he speaks to God's people about God.
2. Online Etymological Dictionary, accessed January 24, 2015, http://www.etymonline.com/index.php?term=retail&allowed_in_frame=0.

3. Online Etymological Dictionary, accessed January 24, 2015, http://www.etymonline.com/index.php?term=faithful&allowed_in_frame=0.
4. Annie J. Flint, "He Giveth More Grace," accessed January 24, 2015, http://nethymnal.org/htm/h/g/hgmgrace.htm.

Chapter 9

1. Compare verses 6–7 with Jeremiah 10:25.
2. Compare verse 3 with 1 Maccabees 7:16.
3. Willem A. VanGemeren, "Psalms" in *The Expositor's Bible Commentary*, vol. 5 (Grand Rapids: Zondervan Publishing House, 1991), 520.
4. Exodus 20:5; 34:14; Deuteronomy 5:9; 6:15; Joshua 24:19; 1 Corinthians 10:22; James 4:5.
5. Wiersbe, *The Bible Exposition Commentary: Wisdom and Poetry*, 234.
6. See Psalm 42:3, 10; 115:2; Joel 2:17; Micah 7:10.
7. Ravi Zacharias, *Walking From East to West* (Grand Rapids: Zondervan, 2006), 67–68.

Chapter 10

1. See Isaiah 5:1–7; Jeremiah 2:21; 6:9; Ezekiel 17:1–24; Hosea 10:1; 14:7
2. Online Etymological Dictionary, accessed January 24 2015, http://www.etymonline.com/index.php?term=refrain. a.
3. Victor P. Hamilton, "שׁוּב (*shob*)," *Theological Wordbook of the Old Testament* (Chicago: Moody Press, 1980), 2:909.

4. Ibid.
5. See Acts 11:18; 2 Timothy 2:25.
6. *My Fair Lady: A Musical Play in Two Acts*. Based on *Pygmalion* by George Bernard Shaw. Adaptation and lyrics by Alan Jay Lerner, Music by Frederick Loewe. (New York: Doward-McCann, Inc., 1956.)
7. The OneCry Movement. http://www.onecry.com/why/declaration/. Accessed January 24, 2015.
8. See NIV, NASB, NLT, NKJV.
9. Online Etymological Dictionary, accessed February 16, 2015, http://www.etymonline.com/index.php?allowed_in_frame=0&search=revive&searchmode=none.

Chapter 11

1. C.S. Lewis, *Reflections on the Psalms* (New York: Harcourt, 1958), 90–95.
2. Ibid.
3. Franz Delitzsch, *Commentary on the Old Testament: Psalms*, vol.5 (Grand Rapids: William B. Eerdmans Publishing Company, reprint 1980), 393.
4. Online Etymological Dictionary, accessed February 16, 2015, http://www.etymonline.com/index.php?allowed_in_frame=0&search=response&searchmode=none.
5. Glen Martin and Gary McIntosh, *The Issachar Factor* (Nashville: Broadman and Holman Publishers, 1993), 199.
6. Boice, *Psalms: An Expositional Commentary*, 2:668.
7. Kidner, *Psalms 73-150*, 2:93.

Chapter 12

1. Not unlike Psalm 50 (chapter 2).
2. Herbert Lockyer, *All the Divine Names and Titles in the Bible* (Grand Rapids: Zondervan Publishing House, 1975), 5.
3. Ibid, 9.
4. Ibid, 7.
5. Associated Press, "Opposition says Putin's lifestyle costs billions," August 28, 2012, http://www.foxnews.com/world/2012/08/28/opposition-says-putin-lifestyle-costs-billions883132/.
6. Dr. Markos made these observations during a lecture given on August 1, 2012 at the Stow Alliance Fellowship, Stow, Ohio.
7. Ibid.
8. Kidner, 2:98, *Psalms 73-150* emphasis added.
9. Lucy Madison, "Obama makes the case for a second term," CBS News, December 12, 2011, http://www.cbsnews.com/8301-503544_162-57341040-503544/obama-makes-the-case-for-a-second-term/.
10. Philip Caufield, "Top basketball prospect Tony Farmer sentenced to 3 years in jail for kidnapping his girlfriend, collapses in court (VIDEO)," *New York Daily News*, August 22, 2012, http://www.nydailynews.com/news/national/top-basketball-prospect-tony-farmer-sentenced-3-years-jail-kidnapping-girlfriend-collapses-court-video-article-1.1142057.

Chapter 13

1. Mark D. Futato, *Cornerstone Biblical Commentary – Volume 7: Psalms and Proverbs* (Carol Stream: Tyndale House Publishers, 2009), 272.
2. VanGemeren, *The Expositor's Bible Commentary*, 5:538.
3. Michael T. Florinsky, *Encyclopedia of Russia and the Soviet Union* (New York: McGraw-Hill, 1961), 258.
4. The History Place, "Genocide in the 20th Century," accessed January 24, 2015, http://www.historyplace.com/worldhistory/genocide/holocaust.htm.
5. All quotes in this paragraph are taken from: http://www.thesixdaywar.org/content/threats.asp. Accessed January 24, 2015
6. Reza Kahlili, "Ayatollah: Kill All Jews, Annihilate Israel," WND.com, February 5, 2015, http://www.wnd.com/2012/02/ayatollah-kill-all-jews-annihilate-israel/.
7. Thomas Erdbrink, "Iran's Vice President Makes Anti-Semitic Speech at Forum," *New York Times*, June 26, 2012, http://www.nytimes.com/2012/06/27/world/middleeast/irans-vice-president-rahimi-makes-anti-semitic-speech.html?_r=0.
8. Colbert I. King, "Iran's anti-Semitism makes it the greatest threat to Jews," *Washington Post*, August 3, 2012, http://www.washingtonpost.com/opinions/colbert-king-irans-anti-semitism-makes-it-the-greatest-threat-to-jews/2012/08/03/75126d28-dcfa-11e1-af1d-753c613ff6d8_story.html.

9. Martin Sherman, "Into the Fray: Reassessing 'root causes' and 'red herrings'," *Jerusalem Post*, October 7, 2011, http://www.jpost.com/Opinion/Columnists/Into-the-Fray-Reassessing-root-causes-and-red-herrings.
10. VanGemeren, *The Expositor's Bible Commentary* 5:536–537.
11. "Praise the Lord," Brown Banister & Mike Hudson ©1978 Word Music, LLC All Rights Reserved. Used By Permission.
12. Leonard J. Coppes, "בָּקַשׁ (*bāqash*)" *Theological Wordbook of the Old Testament*, R. Laird Harris, ed. (Chicago: Moody Press, 1980), 1:126.
13. Kidner, *Psalms 73-105*, 2:302.

CLC
PUBLICATIONS
Fort Washington, PA 19034

This book is published by CLC Publications, an outreach of CLC Ministries International. The purpose of CLC is to make evangelical Christian literature available to all nations so that people may come to faith and maturity in the Lord Jesus Christ. We hope this book has been life changing and has enriched your walk with God through the work of the Holy Spirit. If you would like to know more about CLC, we invite you to visit our website:
www.clcusa.org

To know more about the remarkable story of the founding of CLC International we encourage you to read

LEAP OF FAITH

Norman Grubb

Paperback
Size 5 1/4 x 8, Pages 248
ISBN: 978-0-87508-650-7
ISBN (*e-book*): 978-1-61958-055-8

LONG STORY SHORT

John Kitchen

God has written a grand story—His Story. And He wants you to discover your own story in His. Pastor John Kitchen takes you on a unique journey from Genesis to Revelation, unfolding God's overarching plan so your life can contribute to and move with God's great, eternal Story.

Paperback
Size $5^{1}/_{4}$ x 8, Pages 214
ISBN: 978-1-936143-08-5
ISBN (*e-book*): 978-1-936143-37-5

PRAYING THROUGH

John Kitchen

We pray about our problems and for our needs, but often we don't pray *through*—the deep, intimate kind of prayer that draws hope and healing from God. John Kitchen leads us on a healing journey through the prayers in Psalms and into a more intimate fellowship with our Father.

Paperback
Size 5 1/4 x 8, Pages 261
ISBN: 978-0-87508-978-2
ISBN (*e-book*): 978-1-936143-39-9

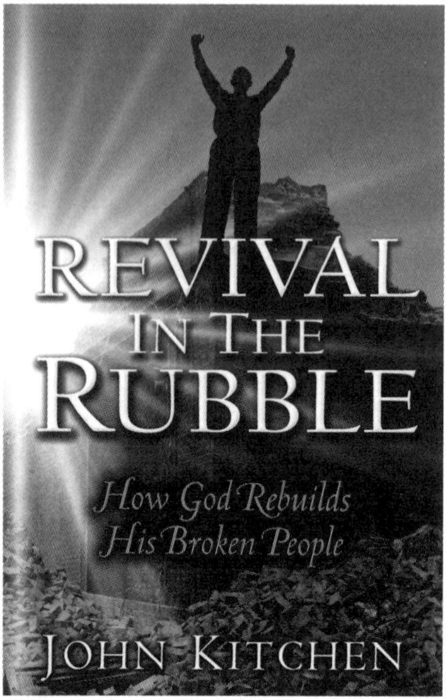

REVIVAL IN THE RUBBLE

John Kitchen

Using the principles found in the book of Nehemiah, John Kitchen shows how personal revival is what God desires for all His people and that it *is* possible. Rising from the rubble of previous generations, revival can happen here and now—if you allow God to work in your life.

Paperback
Size 5 1/4 x 8, Pages 261
ISBN: 978-0-87508-873-0
ISBN (*e-book*): 978-1-61958-034-3